MONTA
HISTOR
HIGHWAY
MARKERS

Headin' for the Hills

The cover art is reproduced from Irvin "Shorty" Shope's painting pictured on the cover of *Headin' for the Hills,* a travel booklet published by the Montana State Highway Department [now the Montana Department of Transportation], Helena, in 1937. It is signed "Irvin Shope, '36."

MONTANA'S HISTORICAL HIGHWAY MARKERS

Second Edition

Compiled by Glenda Clay Bradshaw

From original text by Robert H. Fletcher

Illustrations by Irvin H. "Shorty" Shope

Montana Historical Society Press, Helena

Montana Historical Society Press
225 North Roberts St.
P. O. Box 201201
Helena, Montana 59620-1201

Library of Congress Cataloging-in-Publication Data

Fletcher, Robert H., 1885–1972.
    Montana's historical highway markers / compiled by
Glenda Clay Bradshaw : from original text by Robert H.
Fletcher : illustrations by Irvin H. "Shorty" Shope. — 2nd ed.
      p. cm.
    Includes bibliographical references and index.
    ISBN 0-917298-31-4 (pbk.) : $9.95
    1. Historical markers—Montana—Guidebooks. 2. Auto-
mobile travel—Montana—Guidebooks. 3. Montana—
Guidebooks. 4. Montana—History, Local. I. Bradshaw,
Glenda Clay, 1949—. II. Shope, Irvin. III. Title.
F732.F56 1994   94-20316
917.8604'33—dc20   CIP

CONTENTS

FOREWORD

Montana's history could never be called dull. Having played a major role in the westward expansion of the 1880s, Montana's heritage is a patchwork quilt of Indian peoples on buffalo plains, raucous mining camps and copper kings, cowboys and grass-fat steers, dry-land homesteaders and sod shanties, loggers and freighters. Montanans have always been proud of that history and of those with the gift to recount it. And the telling of that history has assumed many forms over the years. Legends and winter counts told the tales of Montana's first peoples. Later, journals, diaries, and memoirs described the lives of new people on the land. The first-person telling of history—the storyteller—has forever held a place of honor in this land where the articulate speaker, the good talker, has always found a receptive audience.

In 1935, Bob Fletcher convinced the powers-that-be to place road signs throughout Montana at points of historical significance or interest—or at those places that suggested a good story. Fletcher understood the intimacy of Montana history; after all, in 1935, "back then" was not all that long ago. Fletcher's personal acquaintance with many of the men and women who had helped build the state provided more fuel for his idea and supplied him with the stories and the embroidery for the texts that were cut into the original signs.

Aside from being the first such highway markers in the nation, what made them so remarkable was that Bob Fletcher was able to bring folk history to life. Bob's signs spoke in a distinctly Montana voice, using words like "plub" and "larrup" and phrases like "talk medicine" or "head to the tall and uncut" to tell the story. The folklore and the legendry of the state came alive before readers' eyes at or near the sites where the events had taken place.

Using his skills as a storyteller with humor and always an affinity for the land and its peoples, Bob Fletcher told of the dreams, aspirations, successes, failures, and tragedies of Montana. Many Montanans and countless visitors took their first history lessons about the state by reading Bob's signs. Montanans have taken so readily to the road signs that when work was begun in 1986 to refurbish the markers, a hue and cry went out: "Yes, repair the signs and add to them—but don't change the originals!" The signs have become a part of Montana.

Fifty-three years after the historical marker project was completed, Bob Fletcher has found a place in the history of the land he loved most. He was a bit romantic, even nostalgic for "the old days." Yet, his writing and poetry are still a testament to the telling and validation of not just our history but, perhaps more importantly, also the people who made it.

One can only wonder if back in 1935 Bob Fletcher, Shorty Shope, Ace Kindrick, and the Montana Highway Department crew realized what a great contribution they were making to Montana. They might be surprised and pleased to know that we look on their work with the same pride with which they honored other Montanans fifty-three years ago. Bob is gone now, as are Shorty and Ace, but I'd give my best saddle horse if I could see the look on Bob Fletcher's face if he could drive into the Broadus rest stop and see the sign honoring the Montanan who started it all back in 1935.

Michael Korn
Montana Folklife Project

ACKNOWLEDGMENTS

Thanks to all the people who helped track down information on the "old" signs and their creators and on topics for the new markers, including the folks at
> The Montana Historical Society
> The Montana Department of Transportation (in Helena and at the regional offices)
> The Montana Folklife Project
and to all the Montanans around the state who gave their time, talent, and expertise, including Wally McRae, Erva Shope, Richard Shope, Dave Walter, Jim Posewitz, Michael Korn, John Gatchell, Elinor Clack, Betty White, Mick Hager, Tony Incashola and the Flathead Culture Committee, Orville Quick, and Jeff Kindrick. I think of you all each time I drive by one of our signs.

Glenda Bradshaw
Helena, Montana
1989, 1994

Shorty Shope illustrations on pages 1, 5, 13, 14, 29, 45, 47, 70, and 82 are from the Western Life Insurance Company booklet on Shope paintings, n.d. Used with the permission of R. B. Richardson, Helena, Montana.

Shorty Shope illustrations on pages 24, 39, 43, 50, 66, 95, and 97 are from *Local Community History of Valley County, Montana*, published by the Glasgow Women's Club, 1925. Used with the permission of the Montana Federation of Women's Clubs.

Shorty Shope illustrations on pages 7, 9, 17, 28, 88, 89, 93, and 113 are from the Montana Highway Department travel brochure, "Through the Land of the Shining Mountains," by Robert H. Fletcher, n.d. Shope illustrations on the title page and on pages 36, 55, 58, 64, 71, 91, 98, and 114 are from Shope's historical map of Montana produced for the Montana Highway Department.

Illustrations on pages 16, 52, and 77 are from *Historical Markers* by R. H. (Bob) Fletcher, published by the Montana Highway Commission, n.d.

Shorty Shope illustrations on pages 78 and 103 are from a Shope drawing in the collections of the Montana Historical Society, Helena.

The Shope illustration on page 32 is from *Gold* by Robert Fletcher, published by the Union Bank and Trust Company, n.d.

MONTANA HISTORY ON THE ROAD

by Glenda Clay Bradshaw

"A cowboy leaned over in the saddle of his dusty sorrel to read the roadside sign erected on Highway 34 [now state route 287] near old Nevada City. Next to him a sleek sedan with New York license plates pulled up, and the driver leaned out to study the same sign. The cowboy turned to the driver of the sedan. 'Talks turkey, don't it?' he said. 'I never miss one of 'em when I'm travelin' in Montana.'"

Horseback travel is not so common today, fortysome years after this incident was reported in the *Minneapolis Tribune* on May 11, 1947, but thousands of travelers still stop to enjoy the same signs that flank the highways around Montana. They tell the stories of Montana's past and people—the Native Americans; the earliest non-Indian visitors, such as the members of the Lewis and Clark Expedition; fur trappers and explorers; those who came to strike it rich on gold, livestock, and farming; and some of the significant events that happened in the state during the last two hundred years.

The brainchild of Highway Department traffic engineer Bob Fletcher, Montana's historical markers reflect his love of the history of the West and his conviction that history should be made alive and enjoyable. Fletcher, an outgoing, friendly sort, came to Montana in 1908 and for more than a decade worked across the state as a surveyor before joining the Highway Department. During his travels, he met many old-timers who had experienced firsthand some of Montana's early years and others who knew the stories from parents, relatives, or friends who were here "back when."

Fletcher first conceived the idea for historical signs in the 1920s, but it wasn't until 1935 that he was able to convince the Highway Department that it was a winner. "A fancy historical marker is not necessary—just one that attracts the fancy," he explained. He penned colorful stories about Montana's people, places, and events and made them sound as if an old-timer were leaning against your car, reflecting on days gone by. The Highway Department put up about twenty-five signs in 1935 and then waited for indignant reactions to the liberties that Fletcher had taken interpreting the state's past. But the public responded enthusiastically. Both tourists and residents inundated the Highway Department with praise and requests for copies of the sign texts. Even officials from other states wrote for details so they could incorporate some of the markers' design features in their own roadside signs.

The texts of Montana's historical markers even underwent review outside the state. Lewis Gannet of *New Yorker Magazine* praised them in a 1940 column as regional literature: "In Montana the signs are worth reading. . . . So far as I know, these are the only official road signs in any state of America which dare to be light-hearted or colloquial." Historian and essayist Bernard DeVoto also approved in *Harper's Magazine* in 1946: "Montana does its roadside history exhaustively and well. It marks all the important sites—neatly, in excellent taste. What it says about them is accurate, sufficiently generalized to give the unhistorical tourist the idea but sufficiently full and specific for the expert. And its markers use good prose, lightly written, of a humor and realism that exclude the ancestor-worship of the organized descendants of The Pioneers."

World War II correspondent Ernie Pyle liked them as well: "I wish that every state historical society in America would send a delegation to Montana. They might also invite a few writers of history textbooks to go along. And if they would then practice what they learned, I'll bet that twenty years from now we Americans would know a lot more about American history. Montana makes its history a thing of joy instead of a stodgy sermon."

Then he told this story: "One grave fellow got up in the Malta Lions Club and introduced a resolution asking the state highway department to tear the signs down and replace them with something 'dignified.' Unfortunately, the Lions didn't string him to a tree, but they did shout him down."

People also liked the unique roadway design that provided approach signs to warn drivers to slow down, ample pullouts and parking areas, and signs that could be read from a car.

Fletcher stuck with the Highway Department for over thirteen years, writing more than one hundred signs as well as travel brochures and some free-lance history. A few more signs were added to the collection between the 1940s and the mid-1980s.

Two of Fletcher's colleagues in the Highway Department, Shorty Shope and Ace Kindrick, also played essential roles in designing the historical markers. Shope, a fine artist who was a graphic designer for the department, contributed silhouettes of western subjects to embellish the signs. Shope's illustrations run across the top of some signs; on others they decorate the first letter of the text. Like Fletcher, Shope knew many old-timers; he had drawn them and shared their work, riding roundup, herding cattle, roping at branding time. As Fletcher said, "He has conned nature and models in the raw until he can reproduce the West by means of pen and brush with a faithfulness that makes you smell the sage and feel the warm chinook."

The layout and crafting of the markers fell to Ace Kindrick, ramrod of the Highway Department's sign shop. He hand-lettered the earliest signs on plywood; but after finding that these signs weathered too quickly, Kindrick visited the United States Forest Service sign shop in Missoula to observe the routing technique used on their trail signs. Thereafter, he and his signmen hand-routed the letters into thick wooden boards, spray-painted the panels, and then sanded their surfaces, leaving the recessed letters painted. The rest of the signboard was oiled or otherwise finished to enhance the wood's natural grain. Various woods were tried over the years, but redwood became the wood of choice because it weathers well. Most of the signs were hung from wooden crossbeams and posts and set on fieldstone bases.*

In 1985, the 49th Montana Legislature allocated Federal Revenue Sharing money to refurbish the historical markers. Their plan treated Fletcher's writing as artifact and the signs as an element of Montana's historic landscape. Times have changed, however, and some of Fletcher's colorful language is no longer acceptable. Many of his colloquial terms for Montana's first inhabitants ("Injuns," "squaws," "redskins") carry derogatory connotations. Fletcher seems to have meant no disrespect, as this selection from one of his travel brochures indicates: "Today the Montana Indians are on seven reservations. Our highways pass through or near most of them. These tribes produced some mighty fine characters—orators, statesmen, generals, and philosophers. By the way, don't make any personal remarks about an Indian under the delusion that he doesn't savvy. You may be embarrassed. He might haul off and larrup you with some Harvard English. Also, a blanket Indian's outfit doesn't look any more locoed to you than yours does to him. The only difference is that he is too polite to let on."

Earlier intentions aside, sign texts that might be misinterpreted have been edited—but rest assured that the vintage "Fletcher" has been kept as pristine as possible.

Women also might have found offense in a couple of the old historical texts. For example, a quote from road-builder Captain John Mullen advises travelers to ". . . govern them [pack mules] as you would a woman. . . ." This may seem humorous to some; but more important and exciting events transpired on that heavily traveled route and one of them was substituted for the potentially offensive passage. Montana's historical markers form some of travelers' first and firmest impressions of the state and its people. One of the purposes of the markers is to make those impressions positive ones.

---

* The fieldstone bases are disappearing as the Highway Department replaces them with safer, breakaway sign posts. Not as pretty, but easier on vehicles and people in times of collision.

The editing of existing signs and the writing of twenty-three new signs was accomplished during the summer of 1987 as a project shared by the Montana Highway Department and the Montana Historical Society. New signs were cut by a "new-fangled," computer-run router and put up the following fall and winter. Montana's historical roadside markers have been rejuvenated and are on duty.

1994 Note

This book is revised, updated, and printed in a new format for its second edition. Several new signs are entertaining travelers, including the first five in the Native American Historical Markers series that add Native American perspectives to themes that previously were not well represented on historical highway markers. Because they are their own distinct project, the Indian markers are lettered in the order that they were added to the system and they are found in their own section following the numbered markers. The other new markers fall in numerical sequence beginning with number 157.

THE MEN WHO MADE THE SIGNS

Robert H. Fletcher (1885–1972)

Born in Iowa, Bob Fletcher studied mining engineering in Minnesota before coming to Montana in 1908. For several years, surveying work took Fletcher all over the state, enabling him to meet many people and to get an earful of Montana history.

In 1928, Fletcher signed on as plans and traffic engineer for the Montana Highway Department, where he worked for thirteen years. During that time, he wrote creative travel literature, helped establish the port-of-entry stations on arterial highways entering Montana, designed and managed the Montana exhibit at the San Francisco World's Fair, and encouraged the highway department to protect historical and archaeological discoveries, such as Pictograph Caves near Billings. He also devised and implemented the historical markers program.

Robert H. Fletcher
MHS Photograph Archives, Helena

graph Caves near Billings. He also devised and implemented the historical markers program.

Fletcher also became known for his poetry and his free-lance historical writing, which included *Free Grass to Fences,* the story of the Montana cattle range. His best-known verse became the basis for Cole Porter's song, "Don't Fence Me In," part of which is reproduced on a new sign, #137, "Big Sky Country."

Irvin H. "Shorty" Shope (1900–1977)

Born and raised in Boulder, Montana, near his father's small ranch, Shope spent as much time as possible on horseback. After his father's death, the family moved to Missoula where Shope found a mentor in Montana artist Edgar S. Paxson. Shope continued his formal studies in Portland, Oregon, and in New York, finally graduating with a degree in art from the University of Montana in Missoula. He then spent close to ten years working on cattle ranches, studying and drawing scenes of ranch work, western life, and the land.

Irvin H. "Shorty" Shope
MHS Photograph Archives, Helena

In 1925, Shope met cowboy artist Charles M. Russell, who looked through Shope's sketches and encouraged the young painter. On the back of one he wrote, "These drawings of Shope's are all good." Russell also told Shope, who was contemplating attending an eastern art school, "Don't do it, the men, horses and country you love and want to study are out here, not back there."

Bob Fletcher met Shope in 1935 and asked him to draw a historical map of Montana for the Montana Highway Department. Shope became the department's advertising illustrator, creating artwork for travel brochures, signs, and other department literature and drawing western scenes and artifacts to ornament the new roadside historical markers.

Shope started doing free-lance work full-time in 1945, completing hundreds of paintings and twenty-two murals. Shope, one of Montana's best-known and most popular artists, also helped found the Cowboy Artists of America.

Asa T. "Ace" Kindrick (1903–1987)

Born near Seymour, Missouri, Kindrick came to Helena, Montana, with his family in 1914. In 1928, he studied lettering in Detroit, Michigan, and then returned to work in a local automobile and sign shop. The Montana Highway Patrol hired Kindrick to letter their first patrol cars in 1934. The highway department liked his work so well that Kindrick was hired to start a sign shop for them. His employment by the department coincided with the beginning of the historical markers program, and Kindrick put his extraordinary layout and lettering skills to work for Montana history. He directed the highway department sign shop until his retirement in 1969.

Asa T. "Ace" Kindrick
Courtesy of Jeff Kindrick, Helena

HOW TO USE THIS BOOK

This book is not complicated, but a couple of remarks are in order to ease you down the road. The markers are numbered in the order of their creation, which began in 1935. As a result, the history of Montana told on the signs does not appear in chronological or geographical order. To find specific events, people, or places referred to on the signs, see the index.

The quotations from Lewis and Clark's journals have been standardized to conform with the entries found in Gary E. Moulton (through July 27, 1805) and Reuben Gold Thwaites (after July 27, 1805).*

The location of each marker is noted in this book with highway number, nearest mile post marker (MP), and description, such as rest area, city park, or nearest town. The map on the following page shows the sign locations by number or letter. Montana's official highway map is the best reference to use with the book. Maps and vacation planning kits are available free of charge by writing Travel Montana, Department of Commerce, P.O. Box 200533, 1424 9th Avenue, Helena, Montana 59620-0533, or phoning (406) 444-2654 (from Montana) or 1-800-VISIT-MT (from out of state).

---

* Gary E. Moulton, ed.,*The Journals of the Lewis and Clark Expedition*, 8 vols. (Lincoln and London: University of Nebraska Press, 1987); Reuben Gold Thwaites, ed., *Original Journals of the Lewis and Clark Expedition;1804–1806,* vols. (New York: Dodd, Mead & Company, 1904).

HISTORICAL MARKER LOCATIONS

This map is included to show the approximate location of each of the historical markers on Montana's roadways. Using it, you can determine which signs are on your route through the state. It is designed to be useful when you are planning your trip or after your trip, when you recall a sign that you read and want to review what it said.

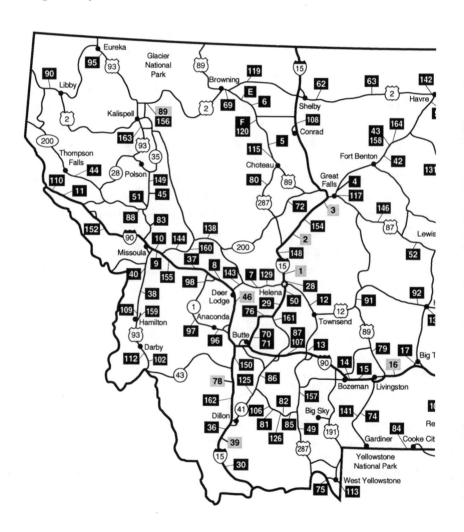

Map Key

65 Each sign's location is indicated by its number, which appears on the map inside a box. When two signs are at the same site they are boxed together.

66 Shaded markers are no longer displayed, though new locations may be found for them in the future.

Note: Several markers are in rest areas that are accessible only from one side of the freeway.

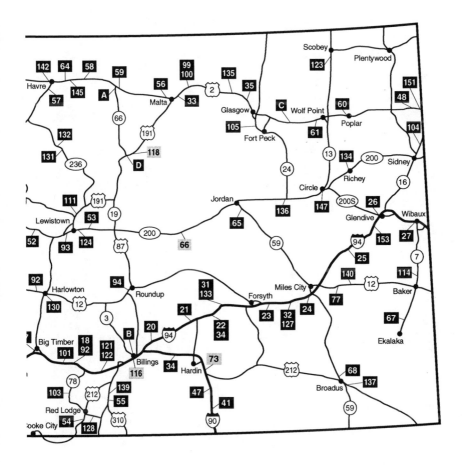

MONTANA'S HISTORICAL HIGHWAY MARKERS

Shope

1. Gates of the Mountains and the Bear Tooth
I-15, MP 209, north of Helena, Exit 29—Marker no longer displayed

Friday, July 19, 1805.

"this evening we entered much the most remarkable clifts that we have yet seen. these clifts rise from the waters edge on either side perpendicularly to the hight of [*about*] 1200 feet....the tow[er]ing and projecting rocks in many places seem ready to tumble on us. the river appears to have forced its way through this immence body of solid rock for the distance of 5¾ Miles and where it makes it's exit below has th[r]own on either side vast collumns of rocks mountains high....it is deep from side to side nor is ther in the 1st 3 miles of this distance a spot except one of a few yards in extent on which a man could rest the soal of his foot....from the singular appearance of this place I called it the *gates of the rocky mountains*" (Extract from Capt. Meriwether Lewis' Diary, Lewis and Clark Expedition).

2. Missouri River Canyon
I-15, MP 239, Dearborn rest area—Marker no longer displayed

The Lewis and Clark Expedition, westward bound, camped just across the river on the night of July 17, 1805. Their equipment was packed in eight canoes. These were rowed, poled, or towed as conditions demanded. Some of the party walked, following an old Indian road through this portion of the canyon. The following morning, as Capt. Lewis recorded in his diary, they ". . . saw a large herd of the Bighorned anamals* on the immencely high and nearly perpendicular clift opposite to us; on the fase of this clift they walked about and bounded from rock to rock with apparent unconcern where it app[e]ared to me that no quadruped could have stood. . . ."

*Mountain sheep

3.   The Sun River

I-15, MP 88, Vaughn way station—Marker no longer displayed

This river was called "The Medicine" by the Indians. On the return trip from the coast Capt. Lewis, of the Lewis and Clark Expedition, struck this river approximately fifty miles west of here. He followed it down to the Missouri passing near this point, July 11, 1806. In his journal under that date he said, "when I arrived in sight of the white-bear Islands the missouri bottoms on both sides of the river were crouded with buffaloe[.] I sincerely beleif that there were not less than 10 thousand buffaloe within a circle of 2 miles arround that place."

The city of Great Falls covers a portion of the plain across which the Expedition made their difficult eighteen-mile portage around the falls of the Missouri in June, 1805.

4.   Black Eagle Falls

River Drive, east of 15th Street Bridge, Great Falls

The uppermost of the Great Falls of the Missouri bears west of this point. The name is a modern one derived from an entry for June 14th, 1805 in the journal of Capt. Meriwether Lewis of the Lewis and Clark Expedition. He discovered the falls on that date and wrote, "... below this fall at a little distance a beautifull little Island well timbered is situated about the middle of the river. in this Island on a Cottonwood tree an Eagle has placed her nest; a more inaccessable spot I believe she could not have found; for neither man nor beast dare pass those gulphs which seperate her little domain from the shores."

After viewing the falls, Capt. Lewis ascended the hill to the former location of the smelter stack and saw "... in these plains and more particularly in the valley just below me immence herds of buffaloe...."

5. Blackfeet and Buffalo
U.S. 89, MP 46, north of Choteau

In the days of the fur traders and trappers immediately
following the time of the Lewis and Clark Expedition
(1804–06) all of this country bordering the Rocky Mountains from here north into Canada and south to the three
forks of the Missouri and to the Yellowstone River was
buffalo range and the hunting grounds of the Blackfeet
Nation. These Indians were fierce and willing fighters who
jealously guarded their territory from invasion.

Like all of the Plains Indians they were dependent
upon the buffalo for their existence. The herds meant meat,
moccasins, robes, leggings and tepees. Board and room on
the hoof. Some Indian legends say that the first buffalo
came out of a hole in the ground. When the seemingly
impossible happened and the buffalo were wiped out there
were Indians who claimed the whites found the spot,
hazed the herds back into it, and plugged the hole.

6. Captain Meriwether Lewis
U.S. 89, MP 85, north of Dupuyer

Captain Meriwether Lewis of the Lewis and Clark Expedition, accompanied by three of his men, explored this portion of the country upon their return trip from the coast. On July 26, 1806, they met eight Piegans (Blackfeet), who Lewis mistakenly identified as Gros Ventres, and camped with them that night on Two Medicine Creek at a point northeast of here. Next morning the Indians, by attempting to steal the explorers' guns and horses, precipitated a fight in which two of the Indians were killed.

This was the only hostile encounter with Indians that the Expedition encountered in their entire trip from St. Louis to the Pacific and back. Lewis unwittingly dropped a bombshell on the Piegans with the news that their traditional enemies, the Nez Perce, Shoshoni and Kootenai, were uniting in an American-inspired peace and would be getting guns and supplies from Yankee traders. This threatened the Blackfeet's 20-year domination of the Northern Plains made possible by Canadian guns.

7. The Mullan Road
U.S. 12, MP 23, McDonald Pass, west of Helena

From this point west to the Idaho line I-90 follows the route of a military road located and constructed during 1858–62 by Captain John Mullan, 2nd Artillery, U.S. Army. The road was 624 miles long and connected Fort Benton, Montana, with Fort Walla Walla, Washington. An average wagon outfit required a minimum of forty-seven days to travel it.

The Captain, aside from his engineering ability, was a man of considerable acumen as evidenced by the following excerpts from his final report. He prophesied "... the locomotive engine will make passage of the ... wild interior at rates of speed which will startle human credulity."

6

Mullan himself might have been incredulous had he seen the freight train that crossed this divide in 1865. Seven camels, each laden with 600 pounds of flour, made the trek from Helena to the Deer Lodge mines. One of the less successful experiments in American transportation history, the dromedary carried tremendous loads, was sure footed, and had great stamina, but the horses, mules and oxen of the teamsters and mule train packers stampeded at the sight and smell of them. The camels were gone from Montana by 1867.

8.　First Discovery of Gold in Montana
I-90, MP 169, Gold Creek rest area

Opposite this point a creek flows into the Clark Fork River from the west. In 1852, a French halfbreed, Francois Finlay, commonly known as "Benetsee," prospected the creek for placer gold. Finlay had some experience in the California goldfields but was inadequately equipped with tools. However, he found colors and in 1858 James and Granville Stuart, Reece Anderson and Thomas Adams, having heard of Benetsee's discovery, prospected the creek. The showing obtained convinced them that there were rich placer mines in Montana. The creek was first called "Benetsee Creek" and afterwards became known as Gold Creek.

The rumors of the strike reached disappointed "Pikes Peakers" as well as the backwash of prospectors from California and resulted in an era of prospecting that uncovered the famous placer deposits of Montana.

9. Junction of the Hell Gate and Big Blackfoot Rivers

Montana 200, west of Milltown

An important Indian road came east through the Hell Gate and turned up the Big Blackfoot. It followed that river almost to its source, then crossed the Continental Divide to the plains country. The Indians called the river the Cokalahishkit, meaning "the river of the road to the buffalo."

Capt. Clark and Capt. Lewis, of the Lewis and Clark Expedition, divided forces near the present site of Missoula on their return trip from the coast. Capt. Lewis and his party followed this Indian road and passed near here July 4th, 1806.

Capt. John Mullan, U.S.A., locator and builder of the Mullan Military Road from Fort Benton to Fort Walla Walla, maintained a construction camp here during the winter of 1861–62 which he named Cantonment Wright. He was the first engineer to bridge the Blackfoot.

10. Hell Gate and Missoula

Old U.S. 10, east of Missoula on I-90 frontage road

In the Indian days the mountain tribes had a road through here which led across the Continental Divide to the buffalo. The Blackfeet, from the plains, used to consider it very sporting to slip into this country on horse-stealing expeditions and to ambush the Nez Perce and Flathead Indians in this narrow part of the canyon. Funeral arrangements were more or less sketchy in those days even amongst friends, so naturally, enemies got very little consideration. In time the place became so cluttered with skulls and bones that it was gruesome enough to make an Indian exclaim "I-sul," expressing surprise and horror. The French trappers elaborated and called it "La Porte d'Enfer" or Gate of Hell.

From these expressions were derived the present-day names Missoula and Hell Gate. If the latter name depresses you it may be encouraging to know that Paradise is just 79 miles northwest of here.

11. Mullan Road
I-90, MP 4, Saltese rest area

During the years 1855–62 Captain John Mullan, 2nd Artillery, U.S.A., located and built what was known as the Mullan Road. Congress authorized the construction of the road under the supervision of the War Department to connect Ft. Benton, the head of navigation on the Missouri, with Ft. Walla Walla, the head of navigation on the Columbia.

In the winter of 1859–60, Capt. Mullan established a winter camp at this point which he called Cantonment Jordan. The Captain had selected this route in preference to the Clark's Fork route because he thought it would have a climatic advantage since it was farther south. However, he later expressed regret for making this choice because investigation showed that the more northerly route was highly favored with chinook winds and the snowfall in consequence was much lighter. The Captain also predicted that both of these routes might eventually be used by transcontinental railroads. His prophesy was correct.

12. Thar's Gold in Them Thar Hills
U.S. 12, MP 69, west of Townsend

The mountains to the west are the Elkhorns. Those to the east across the Canyon Ferry Lake are the Big Belts. Both of these ranges are highly mineralized. Confederate Gulch of the Big Belts was famous in the 1860s for its rich placer diggings. Its Montana Bar, at the old boom camp of Diamond City, now a ghost town, has always been known as "the richest acre of ground in the world." The pay streak ran as high as $2,000 to the pan.

Most of the gulches in the Elkhorns were active as placer camps in the early days and this range is dotted with quartz mines still producing lead, zinc, silver and gold. Like most of the mountains in Montana they have been here a long time.

The Lewis and Clark Expedition came up the Missouri River through this valley in July, 1805.

13. The Three Forks of the Missouri
Old U.S. 10, east of Three Forks

This region was alive with beaver, otter and game before the white man came. It was disputed hunting territory with the Indian tribes. Sacajawea, the Shoshone who guided portions of the Lewis and Clark Expedition, was captured near here when a child, during a battle between her people and the Minnetarees. Her memories of this country were invaluable to the explorers. The Expedition, westward bound, encamped near here for a few days in the latter part of July, 1805. The following year Captain Clark and party came back, July 13, 1806, on their way to explore the Yellowstone River.

In 1808, John Colter, discoverer of Yellowstone Park, and former member of the Lewis and Clark Expedition, was trapping on a stream in this vicinity when captured by a band of Blackfeet. His only companion was killed. Colter was stripped, given a head start, and ordered to run across the flat which was covered with prickly pear. The Indians were hot on his heels but Colter undoubtedly made an all-time record that day for sprints as well as distance events. He outran the Indians over a six-mile course and gained the cover of the timber along the Jefferson River. Once in the stream he dove and came up under a jam of driftwood. This hide-out saved him from a lot of disappointed and mystified Indians. When night came he headed east, weaponless and outnuding the nudists. He traveled in this condition for seven days to Fort Lisa, his headquarters, at the mouth of the Big Horn River.

In 1810, the Missouri Fur Co. built a fur trading post close by but due to the hostility of the Blackfeet Indians were forced to abandon it that fall.

14. Gallatin Valley
Old U.S. 10, east of Bozeman

Captain Wm. Clark, of the Lewis and Clark Expedition, with a party of ten men, passed through this valley July 14, 1806, eastward bound, and guided by the Shoshone woman, Sacajawea. They camped that night at the toe of the mountains on the eastern edge of the valley. Captain Clark wrote in his journal: "I saw Elk, deer and Antelopes, and great deel of old signs of buffalow. their roads is in every direction. . . . emence quantities of beaver on this Fork . . . and their dams very much impeed the navigation of it."

In the early 1860s John Bozeman, young adventurer, and Jim Bridger, grand old man of the mountains, guided rival wagon trains of emigrants and gold-seekers through here over the variously called Bonanza Trail, Bridger Cut-off, or Bozeman Road, from Fort Laramie, Wyo., to Virginia City, Mont. The trail crossed Indian country in direct violation of treaty and was a "cut off" used by impatient pioneers who considered the time saving worth the danger. Traffic was not congested.

11

15. Bozeman Pass

I-90, MP 321, Bozeman Pass

Sacajawea, the Shoshone woman who guided portions of the Lewis and Clark Expedition, led Captain Wm. Clark and his party of ten men over an old buffalo road through this pass on July 15, 1806. They were eastward bound and planned to explore the Yellowstone River to its mouth where they were to rejoin Captain Lewis and party who were returning via the Missouri River.

In the 1860s John M. Bozeman, an adventurous young Georgian, opened a trail from Fort Laramie, Wyoming, to Virginia City, Montana, across the hostile Indian country east of here. He brought his first party through in 1863 and the next year guided a large wagon train of emigrants and gold-seekers over this pass, racing with an outfit in charge of Jim Bridger. Bridger used a pass north of here. These pioneer speed demons made as much as fifteen to twenty miles a day—some days. The outfits reached Virginia City within a few hours of each other.

16. John M. Bozeman

I-90, 14 miles east of Livingston—Marker no longer displayed

John M. Bozeman, the Georgian who pioneered the "cut-off" trail from Fort Laramie, Wyoming to the gold diggin's at Virginia City, Montana, in the early Sixties, was killed up this draw by Blackfeet Indians in April, 1867. He and Tom Coover were on their way to Fort C. F. Smith on the Big Horn River. They had camped on the Yellowstone and Indians stole some of their horses that night. The next day, while Bozeman and Coover were eating, five Indians came into camp with these stolen horses and professed to be friendly Crows. Not until too late were they recognized as Blackfeet by the white men. Without warning they shot and killed Bozeman.* Coover was wounded but escaped.

Bozeman is buried in the town west of here that bears his name.

*Historians doubt the veracity of this version of John Bozeman's death. They now believe that white men disguised as Indians committed the murder.

17. The Bonanza or Bozeman Trail
U.S. 191, west of Big Timber

In the early 1860s there wasn't a ranch in this country from Bismarck to Bozeman and from the Platte River to Canada. To whites it was land considered "fit only to raise Indians" and while some of them were hoping for a crop failure, the majority were indifferent. They didn't care how much the tribes fought amongst themselves. They were like the old-timer whose wife was battling a grizzly bear. He said he never had seen a fight where he took so little interest in the outcome.

Then the white man's greed asserted itself and he looked for a shortcut from the Oregon Trail at Laramie, Wyoming, to the gold diggin's of western Montana. The

Bonanza or Bozeman Trail across Indian hunting grounds was the result. It forded the Yellowstone near here, coming from the southeast. It was a trail soaked with the blood of warriors, soldiers, and immigrants. Thousands of Sioux warriors, primarily under Red Cloud, bolstered by hundreds of Cheyennes and some Arapahos, fought the trail for six years and forced its closure by the Government in 1868.

18.   Captain Wm. Clark
I-90, MP 381, Greycliff rest area

You are now following the historic trail of the Lewis and Clark Expedition. On his return from the Pacific in July 1806, Captain Clark camped for six days about forty miles downstream, near Park City. The Expedition had been looking for timber suitable for building canoes ever since striking the river near Livingston. They found a couple of large cottonwoods here that would serve. They fitted their axes with handles made from chokecherry and went to work making two canoes. When finished they laced them together with a deck of buffalo hides between. Seven men, Sacajawea and her child went curving down the river on this makeshift yacht, arriving at the mouth of the Yellowstone August 3rd. Captain Lewis split off north on the return trip and explored the Marias River and returned via the Missouri, joining them on August 12th.

19. Sacrifice Cliff

Marker no longer displayed.

This sign was removed because of inaccurate information. Sign B in the Indian Historical Markers page 110 has taken its place.

20. Pompey's Pillar

I-94 Frontage Road, MP 25

Captain Wm. Clark, of the Lewis and Clark Expedition, stopped here July 25, 1806, on his way down the Yellowstone. He wrote in his journal that the rock, which he named Pompey's Tower, was: "200 feet high and 400 paces in secumpherance and only axcessable on one side.... The nativs have ingraved on the face of this rock the figures of animals etc. near which I marked my name and the day of the month & year."

The signature is still there. Only fools destroy, but it had to be protected from vandals by a steel screen erected by the Northern Pacific Railway Co.

The party camped a few miles down the Yellowstone that night and the buffalo made so much noise that they had difficulty sleeping.

21. Junction

Town of Custer, Junction City Memorial Park

The frontier town of Junction was just across the Yellowstone River. It was a stage station for outfits heading for old Fort Custer which used to be twenty-five or thirty miles south of here on the Crow Reservation. The original Reservation took in everything in Montana west of the Tongue River and south of the Yellowstone.

There isn't anything left of Junction except a few unkept graves along the hillside but she was lurid in her

days. Calamity Jane sojourned there awhile and helped whoop things up. Calamity was born in Missouri, raised in Virginia City, Montana, and wound up at Deadwood, South Dakota. She had quite a dazzling social career.

Several years ago they found a skeleton of a three-horned dinosaur in the formation which makes the bluffs on the north side of the river. It must have bogged down some time before Junction did—probably a couple of million years.

22. Junction of Big Horn and Yellowstone Rivers
I-94, MPs 42 & 38, Custer rest area

The area which surrounds the mouth of the Big Horn River as it enters the Yellowstone 13 miles east of here is one of the most significant areas in the early history of Montana.

The Yellowstone was known universally to the Indians as Elk River, early French explorers called it Riviere Roche Jaune. The Big Horn was called Le Corne.

Captain William Clark of the Lewis and Clark Expedition, on his return trip from their journey to the Pacific Ocean, camped on the east bank of the Big Horn River, Saturday, July 26th, 1806.

The following year, on November 21st, 1807, an expedition led by Manuel Lisa, a St. Louis fur trader, arrived at the mouth of the Big Horn River. He built a fur trading post which he named Fort Remon in honor of his two-year-old son. This was the first building erected in what is now the State of Montana. From here Lisa sent John Colter to make contact with the Indians who were in winter camp to induce them to come to his post and trade their furs for goods. On this journey Colter discovered the wonders of present-day Yellowstone National Park.

In 1876 during the Sioux and Cheyenne Indian campaign of that year, General Terry and Colonel Gibbon marched up the Big Horn River to the site of Custer's defeat at the Battle of the Little Big Horn. They arrived two days after the battle. The steamer *Far West*, carrying supplies, plied the waters of both rivers and brought the wounded from that encounter back to Fort Abraham Lincoln, Dakota Territory.

23. The Rosebud River
Secondary 446, Far West Park, north of Rosebud

This stream was noted by Captain Wm. Clark, July 28th, 1806, when he was descending the Yellowstone River.

In June, 1876, the columns of General Gibbon and General Custer, both under command of General Terry, met here, the former coming from the west and the latter from the east. They were under orders to campaign against the Sioux and Cheyenne Indians.

The Generals held a conference aboard the supply steamer "Far West" and it was decided that Custer take his column up the Rosebud on a fresh Indian trail which had been found by a scouting party under Major Reno. He started June 22nd. Terry and Gibbon were to proceed to the mouth of the Big Horn and follow that stream up to the valley of the Little Big Horn where they believed the hos-

tiles would be found. Custer was expected to contact
Gibbon June 26th and the two columns would cooperate in
an attack.

Custer reached and attacked the Indian camp June 25th
and his entire command was all but wiped out.

24. The Tongue River
U.S. 12, MP 2, west of Miles City

Captain Wm. Clark, of the Lewis and Clark Expedition,
camped with his party on an island in the Yellowstone,
opposite the mouth of the Tongue, July 29th, 1806. The
Indian name for the river is "Lazeka."

Construction of Fort Keogh, named for one of Custer's
captains killed at the Battle of the Little Big Horn in 1876,
was started in 1877. That knob off to the south is Signal
Butte. During the Indian troubles the army used to flash
sun mirror messages to a post in the Black Hills 175 miles
away. A cloudy day sure threw a lot of static into that
pioneer wireless system.

Miles City, named after General Nelson A. Miles,
started in 1877 as a shack and tent town with a population
running largely to prospectors and miners from the Black
Hills, buffalo hunters, traders and gamblers. She was wild
for a while. When the cattle days of the 1880s arrived many
a Texas trail herd came through here and the city soon
acquired a national reputation as a cattle and horse market
which it has never relinquished.

25. Powder River
Old U.S. 10, MP 14, east of Miles City

This is the river that exuberant parties claim is a mile wide,
an inch deep, and runs uphill. The statement is exagger-
ated. Captain Clark, of the Lewis and Clark Expedition,
named it the Redstone in 1806 and afterwards found out
that the Indians called it the same thing but they pronounced it "Wa-ha-sah." He camped just across the Yellow-

stone from the mouth of the Powder on the night of July 30th, 1806.

Generals Terry and Custer, moving from the east to take part in a campaign against the Sioux and Cheyenne Indians, camped on the Yellowstone about 25 miles west of here June 10, 1876. From that point Major Reno was sent with six troops of the 7th Cavalry to scout the Powder and Tongue valleys for Indian sign. He swung further west and picked up a fresh trail on the Rosebud. It was this trail that led Custer into contact with the hostiles resulting in the Battle of the Little Big Horn.

26. Glendive
Old U.S. 10, MP 326, west of Glendive

A yachting party consisting of Capt. Wm. Clark, of the Lewis and Clark Expedition, six of his men, Sacajawea and her child floated by here August 1, 1806, navigating a craft made by lashing together two hollowed-out cottonwood logs. It was Clark's birthday and the outfit had to land that afternoon to let a herd of buffalo swim the river ahead of them.

Sir George Gore, a "sporting" Irish nobleman, arrived on the scene to hunt in 1855 with Jim Bridger as a guide. Gore's harvest during an eleven-month stay in the Yellowstone Valley included 105 bears, over 2,000 buffalo, and 1,600 elk and deer. He hunted for the thrill of the chase and trophies, only infrequently using the meat. The Crows, who occupied this country, hotly protested the devastation of their food supply.

It was Sir George who named the local tributary to the Yellowstone River "Glendive," and the town assumed the same name 25 years later. During the cattle boom of the 1880s Glendive became the "Queen City of the Cow Land." In 1884, 12,800 "pilgrims" or eastern cattle were unloaded here in one week to help stock the range. They may have been "barnyard stock" but their progeny grew up rough, tough and hard to curry.

27. Pierre Wibaux
Wibaux Park, Wibaux

In 1876, this was strictly buffalo and Indian country. There wasn't a ranch between Bismarck, North Dakota, and Bozeman, Montana. But the U.S. Cavalry rounded up the hostile Indians from 1876 to 1881 and forced them onto reservations while the buffalo hunters were busy clearing the range for the cattle boom of the Eighties.

Pierre Wibaux ran one of the biggest cattle spreads around here in the early days. His will provided a fund to erect a statue of himself "overlooking the land I love so well." It stands a mile west of the town of Wibaux.

From this end of Montana to the west end is just about the same distance as from New York to Chicago. You have to push a lot of ground behind you to get places in this state.

28. Last Chance Gulch
Montana Avenue, north of Custer Avenue, Helena

The city of Helena started as a group of placer miners' cabins and Main Street follows the bottom of Last Chance Gulch. The gulch is formed by the convergence of Oro Fino and Grizzly Gulches and its colorful history began when gold was discovered July 14, 1864, by a party returning to Alder Gulch from an unsuccessful prospecting trip. They agreed to camp and give this locality a try as their "last chance." It proved to be a bonanza.

It is estimated that the Gulch produced thirty millions in pay dirt and there is plenty left beneath the present business district. After a cloudburst, colors and nuggets have been found in the gutters.

Main Street is very irregular in width and alignment. Some opine that it was laid out in this matter to restrict the shooting range of impetuous, hot-blooded gents in the roaring days gone by.

29. Freighters
I-15, MP 178, Jefferson City rest area

Time was when ox and mule teams used to freight along this route. A five-ton truck doesn't look as picturesque but there hasn't been much change in the language of the drivers.

Jerk-line skinners were plumb fluent when addressing their teams. They got right earnest and personal. It was spontaneous—no effort about it. When they got strung out they were worth going a long ways to hear. As a matter of fact you didn't have to go a long ways, providing your hearing was normal. Adjectives came natural to them but they did bog down some on names. They had the same one for each of their string.

Those times have gone forever.

30. Old Trail to the Gold Diggins'
I-15, MP 34, Dell-Redrock rest area

Along in the early 1840s the Americans were like they are now—seething to go somewhere. It got around that Oregon was quite a place. The Iowa people hadn't located California yet. A wagon train pulled out across the plains and made it to Oregon. Then everyone broke out into a rash to be going west.

They packed their prairie schooners with their household goods, gods, and garden tools. Outside of Indians, prairie fires, cholera, famine, cyclones, cloud bursts, quick sand, snow slides, and blizzards they had a tolerably blithe and gay trip.

When gold was found in Montana some of them forked off from the main highway and surged along this trail aiming to reach the rainbow's end. It was mostly one-way traffic but if they did meet a backtracking outfit there was plenty of room to turn out.

31. Yellowstone River Trading Posts
I-94, MP 65, Hysham rest area

Even before the Lewis and Clark Expedition returned to St. Louis in 1806, enterprising traders looked to the upper Missouri and Yellowstone rivers as an unlimited source of furs. At various times between 1807 and 1876, eight trading posts were located between the mouths of the Big Horn and Tongue rivers. Most were owned and operated by the American Fur Company—a firm organized in 1808 by John Jacob Astor. Rather than rely on the rendezvous system and the mountain men, the "Company" built a series of fixed posts designed to encourage the local Native Americans to trade at the forts. The posts included the first Fort Benton (1821), the second Big Horn Post (1824), Fort Cass (1832–1835), Fort Van Buren (1835–1843), Fort Alexander (1842–1850) and two Fort Sarpys. American Fur Company forts were virtual duplicates—each was about 100 square feet with cottonwood palisades and blockhouses at opposite corners. Nearly all the existing accounts of the forts tell stories of a lively trade that was often filled with danger for both trader and Native American. Two of the more well-known people associated with the trading posts were James Beckwourth and Robert Meldrum. The book and motion picture, *A Man Called Horse* was based on Meldrum's experiences among the Crow Indians on the Yellowstone River. By 1876, the fur trade was no longer profitable and the last trading post was abandoned. The trading posts represented a colorful era in the history of Montana. While their presence was fleeting, they significantly impacted the lives of Native Americans and those who chose to garrison these isolated places.

32. Cattle Brands
I-94, MP 112, Hathaway rest area

33. Cattle Brands
U.S. 2, 1.6 Miles east of Malta

CATTLE BRANDS

$\mathcal{M}$any a dogie #(not "doggie" - dudes please note) has been decorated with one of these famous Montana Irons.

CA Running CA	☆ Bug	⋙ Seven VM	⊬ Square & Compass
79 Seventy nine	© Circle C	⊕ Shaving mug	⋃ Quarter circle U
D-S DHS	SH Monogram SH	40 Forty	⌐₂ Lazy H hanging 2
₀8 Three circle	R̄ Bar R	LU LU bar	32 Reversed E 2 bar
H-N N bar N	D Flying D	T Umbrella	♂ Lazy P swinging 9
Y Turkey track	✕ Long X	⊕ Spearhead	Ꮎ Two pole pumpkin
⊿X Hat X	▽ Bull head	∴ Rocking Chair	7-7 Seven bar seven
777 Three sevens	∞ Two dot	⋃ Antler	⊍ Monogram FUF
N̶ N bar	1X Inverted TX	VVV Three V's	= Railroad track
Ψ Pitch fork	⌒ Hash knife	🕱 Hourglass	℉ Monogram PLE
ʃ Fish hook	2A Two A bar	⌂ Rafter circle	Ω Horseshoe bar
⌒ Piece of pie	⌣ Mill Iron	w̲ W bar	◉ Circle diamond
CK	O Circle	U U Lazy J	✠ Maltese cross
IX	LO	707	SL
JO	OW	XIT	WM

#A dogie is a little calf who has lost its mammy and whose daddy has ran off with another cow.

34. Buffalo Country

I-90, MP 476, Hardin rest area, and I-94, MP 42, Custer rest area

35. Buffalo Country

U.S. 2, MP 535, west of Glasgow

Buffalo meant life to the Plains Indians, and the mountain Indians used to slip down from the hills for their share, too. Some tribes would toll buffalo into a concealed corral and then down them; another system was to stampede a herd over a cliff; but the sporting way was to use bows and arrows and ride them down on a trained buffalo horse.

Fat cow was the choice meat. The Indians preserved their meat long before the whites ever had any embalmed beef scandals. They made pemmican by drying and pulverizing the meat, pouring marrow bone grease and oil over it, and packing it away in skin bags. It kept indefinitely, and in food value one pound was worth ten of fresh meat.

Tanned robes and raw-hide were used for bedding, tepees, clothes, war shields, stretchers, travois, canoes, and bags. Horns and bones made tools and utensils. The buffalo

23

played a prominent part in many of their religious rites and jealousy of hereditary hunting grounds brought on most of the intertribal wars.

36. Bannack

I-15, MP 55, Barrett's rest area, southbound

The Lewis and Clark Expedition, westward bound, passed here in August, 1805.

The old mining camp of Bannack is on Grasshopper Creek about twenty miles west of here. The first paying placer discovery in Montana was made in that vicinity by John White, July 28, 1862, and Bannack became the first capital of Montana Territory. They should have built it on wheels. The following spring six prospectors discovered Alder Gulch and practically the entire population of Bannack stampeded to the new diggings where the new camp of Virginia City eventually became the capital until it was changed to Helena.

Henry Plummer, sheriff and secret chief of the road agents, was hanged at Bannack in 1864 by the Vigilantes. It tamed him down considerably.

37. Bearmouth
I-90, MP 143, Bearmouth rest area

Bearmouth, across the river to the south, was a trading point for the placer camps at Beartown, Garnet and Coloma located in the hills north of here. A pioneer family named Lannen operated the gold exchange and a ferryboat.

The river, officially known as Clark Fork of the Columbia and so named for Capt. Wm. Clark of the Lewis and Clark Expedition, has many local names. Its source is Silver Bow Creek, then it becomes the Deer Lodge River, changes to the Hellgate River, is then called the Missoula and winds up as the Clark Fork.

It had one other name given to it by a white man. In September, 1841, the intrepid Jesuit priest, Pierre Jean De Smet, traveled westward through here on his way from St. Louis to establish a mission for the Flathead Indians in the Bitter Root Valley. He crossed the river at the present site of Garrison and named it the St. Ignatius.

38. Fort Owen
U.S. 93, MP 67, Stevensville junction

Between 1831 and 1840 the Flathead Indians sent out three delegations, with St. Louis as their objective, to petition that "Black Robes" be sent to teach them. As a result Father De Smet, a Catholic missionary, established the original St. Mary's Mission here in 1841. He and his assistants hewed logs and built a dwelling, carpenter and blacksmith shops, and a chapel. They drove in the first oxen with wagons, carts, and plows that year and in 1842 brought cows from Colville, Washington, and raised a crop of wheat and garden produce, probably the first in Montana.

In 1843, assisted by Father Ravalli and others, he built the first grist mill. The stones were brought from Antwerp, Belgium, via the Columbia River.

The Mission was sold to Major John Owen in 1850. On its site he built a trading post and fort, the north wall of which stands. The Major was a genial and convivial host when travelers came that way, and for many years Fort Owen was an important trading center for whites as well as Indians.

39. Camp Fortunate

I-15, 20 miles south of Dillon—Marker no longer displayed

In August, 1805, Capt. Lewis, of the Lewis and Clark Expedition, while scouting to the west of here, found a camp of the Shoshone Indians. He had hoped to meet them ever since leaving the Three Forks of the Missouri.

He persuaded their chief and some of the tribe to return to this point with him to meet Capt. Clark, who, with the main body of the Expedition, was coming up the creek with canoes. Clark arrived August 17, 1805.

Sacajawea, who guided portions of the Expedition, had been captured at Three Forks by an enemy tribe when a child. She recognized the Shoshone chief, Cam-e-ah-wah, as her brother. This furthered the friendly relations started by Lewis, and he and Clark were able to secure horses for their outfit from the Indians. They cached their canoes and part of their supplies near here and pulled out towards the West August 24th to cross the Continental Divide.

40. Traveler's Rest

U.S. 93, MP 82, south of Lolo

The Lewis and Clark Expedition, westward bound, camped at the mouth of Lolo Creek September 9th, 10th, 1805. They had been traveling down the Bitter Root Valley

26

and halted here to secure a supply of venison before crossing the mountains to the west via Lolo Pass. They named the spot Traveler's Rest, and it was at this camp that they first learned of the Indian road up Hell Gate leading to the buffalo country east of the main range of the Rockies.

Returning from the coast they again camped here from June 30th, 1806, to July 3rd. When the party divided, Lewis took the Indian "Road to the Buffalo" and after exploring the Marias River descended the Missouri while Clark went via the Big Hole, Beaver Head, Jefferson and Gallatin Valleys and the Yellowstone River.

They reached their rendezvous near the mouth of the Yellowstone within 9 days of each other.

Considering distance and unexplored terrain, they were tolerably punctual.

41.   Fort C. F. Smith

Secondary 313 at Old Fort C. F. Smith turnoff

The ruins of this military post are about 25 miles west of here. In August 1866, two companies of soldiers guided by Jim Bridger established the fort on a plain overlooking the Big Horn River between Spring Gulch and Warrior Creek. It was built of logs and adobe, the third, last and most northerly of three posts built to protect emigrants and freighters on the Bozeman or Bonanza Trail from the Sioux and Cheyennes defending their hunting grounds.

The "Hayfield Fight" occurred August 1st, 1867, three miles east of the fort when a handful of soldiers in a log corral stood off an attacking band of Cheyennes estimated at several hundred strong. The Cheyenne had not anticipated the soldiers' new repeating rifles which were quickly reloadable.

The Sioux under Red Cloud forced the closing of the trail and abandonment of the fort under the Fort Laramie Treaty in 1868. The Indians lost the battle but won the war, though their victory would be short-lived given the ever-increasing encroachment by the settlers.

42. Fort Benton
Off U.S. 87, MP 41, northeast of Fort Benton

Capt. Clark with members of the Lewis and Clark Expedition camped on the site of Fort Benton June 4, 1805.

Originally a trading post of the American Fur Co., it became head of navigation on the Missouri with the arrival of the first steamboat from St. Louis in 1859. She boomed in the early 1860s as a point of entry to the newly discovered placer mines of western Montana. Supplies were freighted out by means of ox teams and profanity.

An early observer states, "Perhaps nowhere else were ever seen motlier crowds of daubed and feathered Indians, buckskin-arrayed half-breed nobility, moccasined trappers, voyageurs, gold seekers and bull drivers . . . on the opening of the boating season. . . ."

43. Marias River
U.S. 87, MP 51, south of Loma

The Lewis and Clark Expedition camped at the mouth of this river just east of here June 3, 1805. Lewis named it Maria's River in honor of his cousin, Miss Maria Wood (over time the apostrophe was dropped). Until exploration proved otherwise, most members of the party believed this river to be the main channel of the Missouri.

On his return trip from the coast in 1806 Capt. Lewis explored the Marias almost to its source.

In the fall of 1831 James Kipp of the American Fur Co. built Fort Piegan at the mouth of the river, as a trading post for the Blackfoot Indians, and acquired 2,400 beaver "plews" or skins by trade during the first 10 days. In 1832 the post was abandoned and the Indians burned it.

44. Thompson Falls
Montana 200, MP 52, east of Thompson Falls

Named for David Thompson, geographer and explorer for the North West Co., a British fur trading outfit.

In November 1809 he built a trading post nearly opposite the mouth of Prospect Creek, named it Selish House, and wintered there.

The Flathead Indians called themselves "Selish," meaning "The People." Like most nations they probably figured they were a little finer haired than the foreigners.

Thompson was the greatest geographer of his day in British America.

The Clark Fork of the Columbia was named for Capt. Wm. Clark of the Lewis and Clark Expedition.

45. Fort Connah

U.S. 93, MP 39, north of St. Ignatius

Fort Connah, the last of the Hudson Bay Co. trading posts established within the present borders of the United States, was built about ¼ mile east of here. Begun by Neil McArthur in fall 1846, his replacement, Angus McDonald, completed it in 1847. It remained an important trading center for the Flatheads until 1871. The old store house is still standing.

Mission Valley was thrown open for settlement in 1910. Prior to that time it was almost entirely virgin prairie, unplowed, unfenced and beautiful to see. You rode a saddle horse to get places. Some people wish it were still like that.

46. Deer Lodge Valley

U.S. 10A, 5 miles east of Deer Lodge—Marker no longer displayed

At the mouth of Rattlesnake Creek, south of Dillon, a phonetic speller erected a road sign in 1862. One side reads

Tu Grass Hop Per digins
30 myle
Kepe the Trale nex the Bluffe

The directions on the other side were a trifle sketchy. They read

Tu JONNI GRANTS
One Hundred and Twenti myle

The placer diggings were at Bannack and the city of Deer Lodge is built on a part of Johnny Grant's ranch. The miners considered Johnny a tolerably close neighbor.

This valley has been a great stock country since the 1850s when said Johnny Grant and friends used to pick up worn-down, foot-sore cattle along the Oregon Trail and haze them up to Montana to rest and fatten.

The mountains to the east are the Continental Divide. Those to the west are the Flint Creek Range.

47. Garryowen

I-90, MP 514, Garryowen

Garryowen, the old Irish tune, was the regimental march-
ing song of the 7th Cavalry, General Custer's command.

The Battle of the Little Big Horn commenced in the
valley just east of here June 25, 1876, after Custer had
ordered Major Marcus A. Reno to move his battalion into
action against the hostile Sioux and Cheyennes, led by
Gall, Crazy Horse, Two Moons and Sitting Bull.

Reno, with 112 men, came out of the hills about 2 ½
miles southeast of here and rode within ¼ mile of the
Indian camp where he was met by the hostiles who out-
numbered the soldiers ten to one. Dismounting his men,
Reno formed a thin skirmish line west across the valley
from the timber along the river. After severe losses he was
forced to retreat to high ground east of the Little Big Horn
where he was joined by Major Benteen's Command. The
combined force stood off the Indians until the approach of
Gibbon's column from the north on the following day
caused the hostiles to pull out. Reno and Benteen were not
aware of Custer's fate until the morning of the 27th.

48. Fort Union

U.S. 2, MP 66, east of Bainville

Fort Union, one of the largest and best known trading
posts of the fur days, was located on the Missouri near the
mouth of the Yellowstone, about 14 miles southeast of
here. Built by the American Fur Company in 1828 for trade
with the Assiniboine Indians, its importance increased
with the arrival of the first steamboat from St. Louis, the
"Yellowstone," about June 17, 1832.

The Blackfeet, influenced by British fur companies, had
refused to trade with Americans until Kenneth McKenzie,
in charge of Ft. Union, succeeded in having a band of this
nation brought to the fort in 1831.

49. Raynold's Pass

U.S. 287, MP 16, Ennis south rest area

The low gap in the mountains on the sky line south of here is Raynold's Pass over the Continental Divide.

Jim Bridger, famous trapper and scout, guided an expedition of scientists through the pass in June of 1860. The party was led by Capt. W. F. Raynolds of the Corps of Engineers, U.S. Army. They came through from the south and camped that night on the Madison River near this point. Capt. Raynolds wrote "The pass is . . . so level that it is difficult to locate the exact point at which the waters divide. I named it Low Pass and deem it to be one of the most remarkable and important features of the topography of the Rocky Mountains."

Jim Bridger didn't savvy road maps or air route beacons but he sure knew his way around.

50. The Prickly Pear Diggings

I-15, Frontage Road, MP 11, south of Montana City

The Fisk or Northern Overland Expedition camped on the future site of Montana City just east of the highway in September, 1862. The outfit consisting of 125 emigrants had left St. Paul June 16, 1862, under the leadership of

Capt. James L. Fisk for the purpose of opening a wagon route to connect at Ft. Benton with the eastern terminal of the Mullan Road from Walla Walla.

They found "Gold Tom," one of Montana's first prospectors, holed up in a tepee near here scratching gravel along Prickly Pear Creek in a search for the rainbow's end. The few colors he was panning out wouldn't have made much of a dent in the national debt, but about half of the Fisk outfit got the gold fever and decided to winter here.

Montana City swaggered into existence in September 1864 as a roaring mining town that is only a memory now. Today it is a suburb of metropolitan Helena.

51. The Mission Valley
U.S. 93, MP 31, St. Ignatius

The Mission Valley, called by the Indians "Place of Encirclement," was occupied by bands of Salish and Kalispel speaking people when the white man came. By treaty with the Government in 1855 it became a part of the reservation of the Confederated Salish and Kootenai Tribes and included some Pend d'Oreille, Kalispel, and Nez Perce.

St. Ignatius Mission, the second built in Montana, was established in 1854 by the Jesuits. The first church was built of whipsawed timber and was held together with wooden pins. Through efforts of the priests the Mission prospered. Four Sisters of Providence from Montreal opened the first school in 1864. The Ursulines arrived in 1890 and opened a school for younger children.

In 1910 the unallotted land on the reservation was thrown open to settlement. The whites and barbed wire moved in.

52. The Judith River
U.S. 87, MP 58, west of Hobson

When the Lewis and Clark Expedition came up the Missouri River in 1805 Capt. Clark named the Judith River for one of the girls he left behind him.

Southwest of here is the Pig-eye Basin and beyond that, in the Little Belt Mountains, is Yogo Gulch. Yogo sapphires are mined there. They are the deepest colored sapphires found in the world and the only ones mined from a lode. When combined with Montana nuggets they make a mighty pretty and unique combination for rings, cuff links, pins and similar fancy doo-dads. Oriental, as well as all other Montana sapphires are found in placer ground.

The Judith Basin country was the early-day stomping ground of Charley M. Russell, famous and beloved Montana cowboy artist. Charley is now camped somewhere across the Great Divide where the grass is good and there aren't any fences.

53. Fort Maginnis
U.S. 87, MP 98, east of Lewistown

Fort Maginnis, the last army post* created in Montana, was built about 8 miles north of here in 1880. This country was great buffalo range before that time but cattlemen were bringing in stock from the western valleys and the Texas longhorns were being trailed in from the southeast. There wasn't room for both cattle and buffalo, so the latter had to go. The soldiers were to protect the cattle from being mistaken for buffalo by hungry Indians, to encourage settlement of the Judith Basin west of here and to patrol the Carroll Road to keep supplies rolling between Carroll (near the mouth of the Musselshell River) and Helena. By 1890 the post was no longer needed, the threatening Indians having been relegated to reservations, and the fort was abandoned with civilian blessings.

There were also quite a number of palefaced parties who were handy with a running iron and prone to make errors as to brands and ownership. Such careless souls were known as "rustlers." Sometimes the cattlemen called on these pariahs with a posse and intimated that they were unpopular. Usually such a visitation cured a rustler or two permanently.

*The last fort established in Montana was not Fort Maginnis. The army established Fort William Henry Harrison near Helena in 1892.

54. The Red Lodge Country
U.S. 212, MP 69, south of Red Lodge

According to tradition, a band of Crow Indians left the main tribe and moved west into the foothills of the Beartooth Range many years ago. They painted their council tepee with red clay and this old-time artistry resulted in the name Red Lodge.

This region is a bonanza for scientists. It is highly fossilized and Nature has opened a book on Beartooth Butte covering about a quarter of a billion years of geological history. It makes pretty snappy reading for parties interested in some of the ologies—palaeontology for example.

Some students opine that prehistoric men existed here several million years earlier than heretofore believed. Personally we don't know, but if there were people prowling around that long ago, of course they would pick Montana as the best place to live.

55. Jim Bridger, Mountain Man
U.S. 310, MP 26, south of Bridger

Jim Bridger arrived in Montana in 1822 as a member of a Rocky Mountain Fur Co. brigade. For years he had no more permanent home than a poker chip. He roamed the entire Rocky Mountain region and often came through this part of the country. A keen observer, a natural geographer and with years of experience amongst the Indians, he became invaluable as a guide and scout for wagon trains and Federal troops following the opening of the Oregon Trail.

He shares honors with John Colter for first discoveries in the Yellowstone Park country. He was prone to elaborate a trifle for the benefit of pilgrims, and it was Jim who embroidered his story of the petrified forest by asserting

that he had seen "a peetrified bird sitting in a peetrified tree, singing a peetrified song."

The Clarks Fork of the Yellowstone was named for Capt. Wm. Clark of the Lewis and Clark Expedition. Chief Joseph led his band of Nez Perce Indians down this river when he made his famous retreat in the summer of 1877.

56. Early Day Outlaws
U.S. 2, MP 467, west of Malta

Take it by and large, the old West produced some tolerably lurid gun toters.

Their hole card was a single-action frontier model .45 Colt, and their long suit was fanning it a split second quicker than similarly inclined gents. This talent sometimes postponed their obsequies quite a while, providing they weren't pushed into taking up rope spinning from the loop end of a lariat by a wearied public. Through choice or force of circumstances these parties sometimes threw in with the "wild bunch—rough riding, shooting hombres, prone to disregard customary respect accorded other people's brands.

Kid Curry's stomping ground in the 1880s was the Little Rockies country about forty miles southwest of here. July 3, 1901, he pulled off a premature Independence Day celebration by holding up the Great Northern No. 3 passenger train and blowing the express car safe near this point. His departure was plumb abrupt. The Great Northern would still probably like to know where he is holed up.

57. Fort Assinniboine
U.S. 87, MP 107, south of Havre

The site of Fort Assinniboine is just east of here. This old military post was established May 9, 1879, and built by the 18th U.S. Infantry under the command of Col. Ruger. The troops were to protect settlers from possible Indian raids following Custer's defeat by the Sioux and Cheyenne tribes and the pursuit of the Nez Perce tribe under Chief Joseph. Fort Assinniboine was a base from which the soldiers could sally forth as a reception committee. No serious Indian disturbance occurred, however.

This post was regarded as one of the most strategic points in the Northwest. The Reserve took in the entire Bears Paw Range of Mountains.

General Pershing served here as a lieutenant under General Miles just prior to the Spanish-American War.

In 1911 the War Department abandoned the post. In 1916 the landless Chippewa and Cree found a home on the southern part of the military reserve when 30,900 acres were set aside as Rocky Boy's Reservation and the state of Montana purchased the fort buildings, the land they stood on, and 2,000 acres which became the Northern Agricultural Research Center of Montana State University (Bozeman). Over sixty years of research have improved land productivity through experiments in dryland farming, crop rotation, summer fallow, shelter-belt plantings, strip farming, improved wheat varieties and livestock research.

58. The Battle of Bears Paw
U.S. 2, MP 403, Chinook

This battle was fought September 30 to October 5, 1877, on Snake Creek, about 20 miles south of here near the Bears Paw Mountains, where after a five days' siege Chief Joseph, one of five remaining Nez Perce leaders, surrendered to Col. Nelson A. Miles of the U.S. Army.

The usual forked-tongue methods of the whites, which had deprived these Indians of their hereditary lands, caused Joseph and six other primary chiefs to lead their people on a tortuous 2000 mile march from their home in Idaho to evade U.S. troops and gain sanctuary in Canada.

These great Indian generals fought against fearful odds. They and their warriors could have escaped by abandoning their women, children and wounded. They refused to do this.

Joseph's courage and care for his people were admired by Col. Miles who promised him safe return to Idaho. One of the blackest records in our dealings with the Indians was the Government's repudiation of this promise and the subsequent treatment accorded Joseph and his followers.

59. Fort Belknap Reservation
U.S. 2, MP 428, rest area

Fort Belknap Reservation was established in 1888 when the Gros Ventres, Blackfeet, and River Crows ceded to the government 17,500,000 acres of their joint reservation that had covered all of northern Montana east of the Rocky Mountains. Home for the Gros Ventres and Assiniboines, who had shared hunting rights on the reservation, it was named for Wm. W. Belknap, secretary of war under President U. S. Grant.

The Gros Ventres (French for "big belly" and pronounced "Grow Von") got the name courtesy of the early French fur trappers. Also known as Atsina, the tribe's own name for themselves is A'a'ninin or "White Clay People." Always a small tribe, they lived in the Red River Valley, North Dakota, from about 1100 to 1400 A.D., then moved west, splitting into two tribes around 1730. One group moved southwest and became the Arapaho, the other northwest, ending up in Montana by the early 1800s. They were close allies to the Blackfeet.

Tradition credits the Assiniboine tribe as separating from the Yanktonai Sioux in the early 1600s. Two of the

first ladies of the tribe, wives of leaders, quarreled over an epicurean delicacy, viz. a buffalo heart. The gentlemen chipped in and the tribe split. One faction headed west and became known as the Assiniboine. They call themselves Nakota, meaning "The Peaceful Ones." When the reservation was created, part of the tribe enrolled here and the remainder at Fort Peck, about 180 miles to the east.

60.   Fort Peck Indian Reservation
U.S. 2, MP 612, city of Poplar

Fort Peck Indian Reservation is the home of two tribes, the Assiniboines, whose forefathers were living in this vicinity when Lewis and Clark came up the Missouri in 1805, and the Dakota (Sioux), descendants of the "hostiles" who fiercely resisted the white invasion of their homelands. Some of the Dakotas took part in the Minnesota uprising of 1862 and moved west when the Army tried to round them up. Others took part in Custer's demise at the Battle of the Little Big Horn in 1876. The Assiniboines, also of

Dakota descent, split from the Yanktonai band in the early 1600s and migrated west. They shared the vast Blackfeet hunting territory set aside by the Treaty of 1855 from which Fort Peck Reservation was created in 1888 when 17,500,000 acres were ceded to the government. Part of the tribe resides on the Fort Belknap Reservation, 160 miles west of here.

Named for Campbell Kennedy Peck, Fort Peck was originally a fur trading post established near the mouth of the Milk River by Abel Farwell for the Durfee and Peck Co. in 1866–67. In 1873, the Bureau of Indian Affairs began using part of the post as Fort Peck Indian Agency. Flooded out by an ice jam on the Missouri in 1877, the agency was moved to the present site at the mouth of the Poplar River. The earlier site now rests under the waters behind Fort Peck Dam.

61. Wolf Point
U.S. 2, MP 590, west of Wolf Point

The Lewis and Clark Expedition passed here, westward bound in 1805. Fur trappers and traders followed a few years later. Steamboats began making it from St. Louis up the Missouri as far as Fort Benton in the early 1860s and this was considered the halfway point between Bismarck and Fort Benton. Wood choppers supplied cord wood for boats stopping to refuel. An American Fur Company packet burned and blew up in 1861 not far from here. A deck hand tapped a barrel of alcohol by candle light with a gimlet. The fumes, the candle, and 25 kegs of powder did the rest.

This district was favorite buffalo country for the Assiniboines and Sioux.

A party of trappers poisoned several hundred wolves one winter, hauled the frozen carcasses in and stacked them until spring for skinning. It taught the varmints a lesson. No one in Wolf Point has been bothered by a wolf at the door since then.

62. The Oily Boid Gets the Woim
U.S. 2, MP 282, east of Shelby

A narrow gauge railroad nicknamed the "turkey track" used to connect Great Falls, Montana, and Lethbridge, Alberta. When the main line of the Great Northern crossed it in 1891, Shelby Junction came into existence. The hills and plains around here were cow country. The Junction became an oasis where parched cowpunchers cauterized their tonsils with forty-rod and grew plumb irresponsible and ebullient.

In 1910 the dry-landers began homesteading. They built fences and plowed under the native grass. The days of open range were gone. Shelby quit her swaggering frontier ways and became concrete sidewalk and sewer system conscious.

Dry land farming didn't turn out to be such a profitable endeavor but in 1921 geologists discovered that this country had an ace in the hole. Oil was struck between here and the Canadian line, and the town boomed again.

63. The Sweet Grass Hills
U.S. 2, MP 327, east of Chester

You can see the Sweet Grass Hills or the Three Buttes to the north of here on a reasonably clear day. The Indians used them as watch towers from which they could locate buffalo herds. Things sure grow in this country. Some old timers claim that when they arrived those buttes weren't much bigger than prairie dog mounds.

In 1884 a Blackfoot Indian found gold in them thar hills and the usual stampede followed. The middle peak is called Gold Butte. It was claimed that the placer ground in Two Bits Gulch produced twenty-five cents in colors for every shovel full of gravel.

The pay dirt has been pretty well worked out and the glamour of boom days is gone, but a few old-timers still prospect the gulches, hoping some day to find that elusive pot of gold at the rainbow's end, called the Mother Lode.

64. Havre

U.S. 2, MP 385, east of Havre

Cowpunchers, miners, and soldiers are tolerably virile persons as a rule. When they went to town in the frontier days seeking surcease from vocational cares and solace in the cup that cheers it was just as well for the urbanites to either brace themselves or take to cover. The citizens of any town willing and able to be host city for a combination of the above diamonds in the rough had to be quick on the draw and used to inhaling powder smoke.

Havre came into existence as a division point when the Great Northern Railroad was built and purveyed pastime to cowboys, doughboys and miners on the side. It is hard to believe now, but as a frontier camp, she was wild and hard to curry.

65. Indian Country

Montana 22, MP 83, south of Jordan

Until the early 1880s this portion of Montana was wild unsettled country where roving parties of Sioux, Crow and Assiniboine Indians hunted buffalo and clashed in tribal warfare. Sitting Bull's band of Hunkpapa Sioux frequently ranged through here and except for a few nomadic trappers there were no white men.

With the coming of the Texas trail herds the buffalo were slaughtered to clear the range for beef critters and the cattle kings held sway for many years.

In 1910 the first wave of homesteaders surged in and the open range dwindled before their fences and plowed fields. The glamour of the frontier days is gone.

66. Fort Musselshell

Montana 200, 1.5 miles east of Mosby—Marker no longer displayed

Fort Musselshell was located on the Missouri River about 35 miles north of here. It was a trading post in the 1860s and 1870s and as such had a brief but colorful career. The only whites in that part of the state were woodchoppers for the Missouri River steamboats, wolfers, trappers and Indian traders.

The River Crows and Gros Ventre Indians traded there. A buffalo robe brought them 3 cups of coffee, or 6 cups of sugar, or 10 cups of flour. It was tolerably profitable business from the trader's standpoint. The Assiniboines and Sioux regarded this post as an amusement center where bands of ambitious warriors could lie in ambush and get target practice on careless whites.

During the cattle days of the 1880s the mouth of the Musselshell became a cattle rustler's hangout but after a Vigilance Committee stretched a few of them they seemed to lose interest.

67. Ekalaka
Montana 7, MP 1, north of Ekalaka

Some people claim an old buffalo hunter figured that starting a thirst emporium for parched cowpunchers on this end of the range would furnish him a more lucrative and interesting vocation than downing buffalo. He picked a location and was hauling a load of logs to erect this

proposed edifice for the eradication of ennui when he bogged down in a snowdrift. "Hell," he exclaimed, "Any place in Montana is a good place for a saloon," so he unloaded and built her right there. That was the traditional start of Ekalaka in the 1860s and the old undaunted pioneer spirit of the West still lingers here.

When it became a town it was named after an Indian girl, born on the Powder River, who was the daughter of Eagle Man, an Ogalala Sioux. She was a niece of the War Chief, Red Cloud, and was also related to Sitting Bull. She became the wife of David H. Russell, the first white man to settle permanently in this locality.

68. Southeastern Montana
U.S. 212, MP 79, Broadus

The first white man to enter Montana was Pierre de La Verendrye, a French explorer, who arrived in this corner of the state on New Year's Day, 1743. His party had traveled southwest from a Canadian fur trading post to investigate Indian tales of the Land of the Shining Mountains.

Next came the trappers, following the Lewis and Clark Expedition of 1804–06. Like the rest of Montana east of the mountains this portion remained unsettled Indian and buffalo country until the Texas trail herds overran the range in the 1880s. Up to that time it was a favorite hunting ground for roving bands of Cheyenne Indians and the various Sioux tribes.

With the coming of the cow-man the buffalo gave way to the beef critter and high-heeled boots replaced buckskin moccasins.

69. The Blackfeet Nation
U.S. 2, MP 224, east of Browning

The Blackfeet Nation consists of three tribes, the Pikunis or Piegans, the Bloods and the Blackfoot. Each tribe is di-

Shope

vided into clans marking blood relationship. The majority of the Indians on this reservation are Piegans.

Many years ago the Blackfeet ranged from north of Edmonton, Alberta to the Yellowstone River. They were quick to resent and avenge insult or wrong, but powerful and loyal allies when their friendship was won.

They were greatly feared by early trappers and settlers because of the vigor with which they defended their hereditary hunting grounds from encroachment.

No tribe ever exceeded them in bravery. Proud of their lineage and history they have jealously preserved their tribal customs and traditions. They have produced great orators, artists, and statesmen.

The Government record of the sign language of all American Indians, started by the late General Hugh L. Scott, was completed by the late Richard Sanderville, who was official interpreter of this reservation.

70. Butte

I-15, MP 130, overlook north of Butte

The "greatest mining camp on earth" built on "the richest hill in the world." That hill, which has produced over two billion dollars worth of gold, silver, copper and zinc, is literally honeycombed with drifts, winzes and stopes that extend beneath the city. There are over 3,000 miles of workings, and shafts reach a depth of 4,000 feet.

This immediate country was opened as a placer district in 1864. Later Butte became a quartz mining camp and successively opened silver, copper and zinc deposits.

Butte has a most cosmopolitan population derived from the four corners of the world. She was a bold, unashamed, rootin', tootin', hell-roarin' camp in days gone by and still drinks her liquor straight.

71. Meaderville

I-15, MP 130, overlook north of Butte

William Allison and G. O. Humphreys had the Butte hill, richest hill on earth, entirely to themselves when they located their first quartz claims there in 1864.

They discovered an abandoned prospect hole which had evidently been dug by unknown miners a number of years before. These mysterious prospectors had used elk horn tines for gads, and broken bits of these primitive tools were found around the shafts. Allison and Humphreys died, their property passed into other hands, and they never knew that they were the potential owners of untold wealth.

Meaderville was named for Charles T. Meader, a fortyniner who went to California via Cape Horn and who came to Butte in 1876.

72. Fort Shaw

Montana 200, MP 133, west of Fort Shaw

Barring fur trading posts, the first important white settlements in Montana were the mining camps in the western

mountains. Everything to the east belonged to the plains Indians and was buffalo range. To protect the miners and settlers from possible incursions of hostile tribes, a series of military posts was established around the eastern border of the mining camps and settlements. Fort Shaw, established in 1867, was one of these. It also protected the stage and freight trail from Fort Benton, head of navigation on the Missouri, to the Last Chance Gulch placer diggings at Helena. Everything north of the Sun River was Blackfeet Indian Territory at that time. The fort was built by the 13th U.S. Infantry, under Major Wm. Clinton.

General Gibbon led his troops from here in 1876 to join General Terry and General Custer on the Yellowstone just prior to the latter's disastrous fight with the Sioux and Cheyenne Indians at the Battle of the Little Big Horn.

73. The Crow Indians
I-90, Crow Agency—Marker no longer displayed

"Crow" is the white man's mistaken interpretation of the Indian name Ab-saro-ka, meaning "bird" or "thing that flies." The nation divided into two tribes, the River and the Mountain Crows. In frontier days they warred with the Sioux and Blackfeet on the north and east and were usually friendly with the Nez Perce and Flatheads from the west. They were accomplished horse thieves and kept themselves well provided with ponies. Horse stealing was a highly honorable and adventurous practice amongst the western Indians.

Never bitterly opposed to the whites, many of their warriors served as scouts for the U.S. Army in their campaigns against hostile tribes.

Their great chief, Plenty Coups, was chosen as the representative of all the American Indians to place their wreath on the tomb of the Unknown Soldier at Arlington.

74. Emigrant Gulch
U.S. 89, MP 28, north of Gardiner

A party of emigrants who had traveled with a wagon train across the plains via the Bozeman or Bonanza Trail arrived in this gulch August 28, 1864. Two days later three of these men explored the upper and more inaccessible portion of the gulch and struck good pay. A mining boom followed.

When cold weather froze the sluices the miners moved down to the valley, built cabins and "Yellowstone City" began its brief career. Provisions were scarce that winter. Flour sold for $28 per 96 lb. sack, while smoking tobacco was literally worth its weight in gold.

The strike was not a fabulous one, but snug stakes rewarded many of the pioneers for their energy and hardships.

75. Targhee Pass
U.S. 20, MP 0, west of West Yellowstone

This pass across the Continental Divide takes its name from an early-day Bannack Chief. Free trappers and fur brigades of the Missouri River and Rocky Mountain Fur companies were familiar with the surrounding country in the early part of the last century.

Chief Joseph led his band of Nez Perce Indians through this pass in 1877 while making his famous 2,000-mile march from the central Idaho country in an effort to evade

U.S. troops and find sanctuary in Canada. He was closely followed through the pass by the pursuing forces of General Howard. Joseph repulsed or out-distanced all the commands sent against him until finally forced to surrender to Col. Nelson A. Miles at the Battle of the Bear's Paw, when within a comparatively few miles of the Canadian line.

76. Mining Country
I-15 Frontage Road, MP 0, north of Basin

This is about the center of a rich mining district extending from Butte to Helena. The mountains are spurs of the Continental Divide.

Ghost and active mining camps are to be found in almost every gulch. The ores yield gold, silver, copper, lead and zinc. The district has been producing since quartz mining came into favor following the first wave of placer mining in the 1860s. In those days placer deposits were the poor man's eldorado. They needed little more than a grub stake, a pick and a shovel to work them. Quartz properties, seldom rich at the surface, required machinery and capital, transportation and smelting facilities.

Before smelters were built in Montana, ore from some of the richest mines in this region was shipped by freight team, boat and rail to Swansea, Wales, and Freiburg, Germany, for treatment.

77. Powder River
U.S. 12, MP 32, east of Miles City

When a top rider from this part of the country is forking the hurricane deck of a sun-fishing, fuzz-tail, some of his pals are prone to sit on the rope rail of the corral, emitting advice and hollering "Powder River! Let 'er buck!!" by way of encouragement. The 91st Division adopted that war cry

during the first World War
and spread it far and wide.
Well, this is the famous
Powder River, that enthu-
siasts allege is a "mile
wide, an inch deep, and
runs up hill."

The entire Powder
River country was favorite
buffalo hunting range for
the Sioux and Cheyenne
Indians before the day of
cattle men. Many inter-
tribal battles were fought
in this region as well as
frequent skirmishes be-
tween Indians and the U.S.
troops. The country is rich
in Indian lore and tales of
the subsequent reign of the
cattle kings.

78. The Big Hole River
I-15, 2 miles north of Melrose—Marker no longer
displayed

This stream was named the Wisdom River by Captains
Lewis and Clark. Their expedition, westward bound,
passed its mouth Aug. 4, 1805. "Hole" was a term frequently used by the fur trappers in the early part of the
last century to designate a mountain valley. An extensive
valley west of here drained by this river became known as
"The Big Hole" and the name of the river was changed
accordingly.

The Battle of the Big Hole was fought Aug. 9, 1877, in
the valley just mentioned. Chief Joseph's band of fugitive
Nez Perce Indians repulsed U.S. troops under command of
General Gibbon.

79. Shields River Valley
U.S. 89, MP 24, south of Wilsall

This river was named by Capt. Wm. Clark of the Lewis and Clark Expedition in honor of John Shields, a member of the party. Capt. Clark and his men, guided by Sacajawea, the Shoshone woman, camped at the mouth of the river July 15, 1806, while exploring the Yellowstone on their return trip from the coast.

Jim Bridger, famous trapper, trader and scout, guided emigrant wagon trains from Fort Laramie, Wyoming, to Virginia City, Montana, in the 1860s, crossing hostile Indian country via the Bonanza Trail. Bridger's route came up this valley from the Yellowstone, followed up Brackett Creek, crossed the divide west of here to strike Bridger Creek and thence down the latter to the Gallatin Valley.

80. Sun River
U.S. 287, MP 42, north of Augusta

The Sun River was called the Medicine River by the Indians in the days of the Lewis and Clark Expedition (1804–06). The Indian name was probably given because of an unusual mineral deposit possessing marked medicinal properties which exist in a side gulch of the Sun River Canyon west of here.

This country was claimed and occupied by the Blackfeet Nation in the frontier days. After the Indians were relegated to reservations it became cattle range.

In 1913 the U.S. Reclamation Service built a storage and diversion dam near the mouth of the canyon and the water is used for irrigation on the valleys and bench lands east of here.

81. The Ruby Valley
Montana 287, MP 22, near Alder

The Ruby River was called the Passamari by the Indians and became known as the Stinking Water to the whites in the pioneer days. It joins the Beaverhead to form the Jefferson Fork of the Missouri.

Fur trappers, Indians, prospectors and road agents have ridden the trails through here in days gone by.

The large gravel piles to the west are the tailings resulting from gold dredging operations over about a twenty-year period beginning in 1899. The dredges are reported to have recovered between eight and nine million dollars in gold from the floor of the valley and the lower end of Alder Gulch.

82. Nevada City
Montana 287, MP 16, at Nevada City

A ghost town now, but once one of the hell roarin' mining camps that lined Alder Gulch in the 1860s. It was a trading point where gold dust and nuggets were the medium of exchange: where men were men and women were scarce. A stack of whites cost twenty, the sky was the limit and everyone was heeled.

The first Vigilante execution took place here when George Ives, notorious road agent, was convicted of murder and hanged.

The gulch was once filled with romance, glamour, melodrama, comedy and tragedy. It's plumb peaceful now.

83. The Jocko Valley
U.S. 93, MP 14, south of Arlee

Named for Jacco (Jacques) Raphael Finlay, a fur trader and trapper in the Kootenai and Flathead Indian country, 1806–09.

By treaty of Aug. 27, 1872, the Flathead Indians were supposed to have relinquished claim to their hereditary lands in the Bitter Root Valley, accepting the present reservation in lieu thereof. Charlot, head chief of the Flatheads, always denied signing the treaty although when the papers were filed in Washington his name appeared on them, possibly a forgery.

Arlee (pronounced Ah-lee by the Indians) was a war chief and did sign the treaty so the Government recognized him thereafter as head chief. Charlot never spoke to him afterwards.

84. Cooke City
U.S. 212, MP 3, west of Cooke City

In 1868 a party of prospectors came into this country by way of Soda Butte Creek. They found rich float but were set afoot by Indians. Caching their surplus supplies on the stream now called Cache Creek, they made it back to the Yellowstone and reported their find. In the next few years many prospectors combed these mountains; the first real development began about 1880 with Jay Cooke's infusion of eastern capital.

Chief Joseph's band of fugitive Nez Perce Indians came through here in 1877. In 1883 there were 135 log cabins in the settlement, two general stores and thirteen saloons.

Cooke City had been waiting years for reasonable transportation connections to the outside world so that her promising ore deposits could be profitably mined. She's no blushing maiden, but this highway was the answer to her prayers.

85. Virginia City
Montana 287, MP 14, near Virginia City

All of Montana has the deepest pride and affection for Virginia City. No more colorful pioneer mining camp ever existed. Dramatic tales of the early days in this vicinity are legion.

Rich placer diggin's were discovered in Alder Gulch in the spring of 1863 and the stampede of gold-seekers and their parasites was on. Sluices soon lined the gulch and various "cities" blossomed forth as trading and amusement centers for free-handed miners. Virginia City, best known of these and the sole survivor, became the Capital of the Territory. Pioneers, who with their descendants were to mold the destinies of the state, were among its first citizens. If you like true stories more picturesque than fiction, Virginia City and Alder Gulch can furnish them in countless numbers.

86. Jefferson Valley
Montana 41, MP 47, north of Twin Bridges

The Lewis and Clark Expedition, westward bound, came up the Jefferson River in August, 1805. They were hoping to find the Shoshone Indians, Sacajawea's tribe, and trade for horses to use in crossing the mountains west of here. Just south of here the river forks, the east fork being the Ruby and the west fork the Beaverhead. They followed the latter and met the Shoshones near Armstead, which is now under the Clark Canyon Reservoir 20 miles south of Dillon.

On the return trip from the coast in 1806, Capt. Wm. Clark retraced their former route down this valley to Three Forks, and then crossed the Yellowstone. Capt. Lewis left Clark in the Bitter Root Valley, crossed the Divide via the

Big Blackfoot River and thence to Great Falls. They met near the mouth of the Yellowstone, arriving within nine days of each other.

87. Father De Smet
Old U.S. 10, MP 3, east of Whitehall

The Lewis and Clark Expedition passed here, westward bound, August 2, 1805. Captain Lewis named the Boulder River "Fields Creek" for one of the party.

In August, 1840, Pierre Jean De Smet, S.J., a Catholic missionary of Belgian birth, camped near the mouth of the Boulder River with the Flathead Indians and celebrated the holy sacrifice of the Mass. Father De Smet left the Indians soon after to go to St. Louis. He returned the following year and established the original St. Mary's Mission in the Bitter Root Valley, hereditary home of the Flatheads. Fearless and zealous, his many experiences during the pioneer days have been chronicled and form a most interesting chapter in the frontier annals of Montana.

88. Flathead Reservation
Montana 200, MP 116, west of Ravalli

The Native Americans on this reservation belong to the Salish, Kalispel, Spokane, Kootenai and Pend d'Oreille tribes. Lewis and Clark met the Salish in 1805 and described them and their allies, the Nez Perce, as being friendly and exceptional people. "Flathead" was a misnomer applied to the Salish by Lewis and Clark. No one knows for sure where it came from, but like many early

names for tribes, it stuck. It seems that the whites almost always had a handle to hang on a tribe before they met anyone who could tell them their own name for themselves.

The Flatheads frequently crossed the mountains to the plains to hunt buffalo and there clash with the Blackfeet, their hereditary enemies. Many of the French and Scotch names amongst them came from marriage with the Hudson Bay Co. trappers and traders in the early fur days.

89. Bad Rock Canyon
U.S. 2, MP 141, east of Columbia Falls—Marker no longer displayed.

Text deleted due to inaccuracy.

90. Kootenai River
U.S. 2, MP 21, west of Libby

The river is named for the Kootenai tribe that lived and hunted in this part of Montana and adjoining territory in Idaho and Canada. They were settled south of Flathead Lake in 1855 with the Salish on the Flathead Reservation.

They were friendly with neighboring mountain tribes but suffered frequently from the incursions of their bitter enemies, the Blackfeet, who came across the Continental Divide from the plains on horse-stealing and scalp-raising expeditions.

First white men in here were trappers and traders for British fur companies as early as 1809. Placer discoveries were made and mining operations commenced about sixty years later.

91. The Smith River Valley
U.S. 89, MP 34, south of White Sulphur Springs

The mountains to the west are the Big Belts, and those to the east are the Castle Mountains. The gulches draining the west slope of the Big Belts were famous in the 1860s and 1870s for their gold placer diggings. Montana Bar in Confederate Gulch was called the "richest acre of ground in the world." The Castle Mountains are also well-known for their quartz mines.

Fort Logan, first established as Camp Baker in November, 1869, as a military outpost to protect the mining camps and ranches to the west from possible attack by Indians, was located towards the north end of the valley. The White Sulphur Springs, typical of the many thermal springs in Montana, were discovered in 1866 by Jas. Scott Brewer. Analysis of the water is said to be almost identical with that at the famous spa, Baden Baden, Germany.

92. The Crazy Mountains
U.S. 12, MP 95, west of Harlowton and I-90, MP 381, Greycliff rest area

The Crazy Mountains, which you can see to the southwest [northwest from I-90 location], are an outlying range. They are far more rugged and beautiful than they appear at a distance. The story goes that a woman traveling across the plains with a wagon train of emigrants went insane. She escaped from the party and was found near these mountains. So they were called the Crazy Woman Mountains, which in time was shortened.

This district was great cow country in the days of the open range, and there are still a number of large cattle ranches in this vicinity, though under fence. The town of Two Dot gets its name from an early day brand.

93. The Judith Basin Country
U.S. 87, MP 81, west of Lewistown

The first white man to explore this district was Hugh Monroe, called "Rising Wolf" by the Blackfeet Indians. The Judith Basin was favorite hunting ground for this Nation, and Monroe, as an adopted member of the Piegan Tribe, often came here with them during the first half of the last century.

Reed's Fort, a typical Indian trading post, was located near here. Operated by Major Reed and Jim Bowles, the latter a friend of Jim Bridger, the post was going strong during the 1870s.

In the early 1880s cattlemen and prospectors moved in. Rich mines were opened in the Judith Mountains and range stock replaced the vanishing buffalo. This country is rich in frontier history and tales of the pioneers.

94. Cow Country
U.S. 12, MP 167, west of Roundup

In the 1880s—days of the open range—many a roundup outfit worked this country. The spring roundup gathered the cattle in order to brand and tally the calf crop. The fall roundup gathered beef critters for shipping.

An outfit consisted of the captain, the riders, the "reps" from neighboring ranges, the cavvy or horse herd in charge of the day herder and night hawk, the four horse chuck wagon piloted by the cook and the bed wagon driven by his flunkey. Camp moved each day.

The cowboys rode circle in the morning, combing the breaks and coulees for cattle and heading them toward the central point to form a herd. In the afternoons of spring roundup the guards kept the herd together, the cutters split out the cows with calves, the ropers dabbed their loops on the calves, took a couple of dally welts around the saddle horn and dragged 'em to the fire. There the calf wrestlers flanked and flopped them and the brander decorated them with ear notches, or dew laps, and a hot iron. It wasn't all sunshine and roses.

95. Tobacco Plains
U.S. 93, MP 178, east of Eureka

During the fur trapping and trading days in the early part
of the last century this corner of the state was remote and
inaccessible from the customary trapping grounds and
operating bases of the Americans. Representatives of the
British and Canadian companies came in from the north
and established posts along the Kootenai River.

The Tobacco Plains were so named by the Indians who
planted tobacco for religious uses.

In prehistoric times the valley of the Kootenai was filled
with an enormous ice sheet.

96. Anaconda
U.S. 1, east edge of Anaconda

Selected by Marcus Daly as a smelter site in 1883 because of
an abundant supply of good water, Anaconda was the
home of the Washoe Smelter of the Anaconda Copper
Mining Company until 1980. History has been made here in
the science of copper smelting, and the plant is famous
throughout the mining and metallurgical world.

From a straggling tent town Anaconda grew to be a
modern city, but retained all of the aggressive spirit of the
pioneer days. This spirit refused to die with the Anaconda
Co. pull-out and the town remains a vital community.

97. Atlantic Cable Quartz Lode
U.S. 10A, MP 20, west of Anaconda

This mining property was located June 15, 1867, the name
commemorating the laying of the second transatlantic
cable.

The locators were Alexander Aiken, John B. Pearson and
Jonas Stough. They were camped on Flint Creek and their
horses drifted off. In tracking them to this vicinity the men
found float that led to the discovery.

Machinery for the first mill was imported from Swansea, Wales, and freighted by team from Corinne, Utah, the nearest railroad point.

The mine was operated with indifferent success until about 1880 when extremely rich ore was opened up—a 500 ft. piece of ground producing $6,500,000 in gold. W. A. Clark paid $10,000 for one chunk of ore taken from this mine in 1889 and claimed it was the largest gold nugget ever found.

98. Southern Flint Creek Valley
U.S. 10A, MP 57, south of Hall

Lured by the glitter of gold along the Henderson Gulch terrain the prospector and placer miner flocked to southern Flint Creek Valley not only to extract the precious metal, but to develop a country rich in agricultural wealth. The verdant beauty of this valley of the Flint Creek is a lasting monument to pioneer vision and enterprise. A scion of a pioneer family—Mrs. Julia Byrne Hall (wife of Harry Hall)—gave her name to the town of Hall whilst 1891 saw the beginnings of the building in the Stone Station district of the religious edifice that afterwards became known as St. Michael's.

99. The Cree Crossing
U.S. 2, MP 490, east of Malta

The Milk River, which flows through this prehistoric valley of the Missouri now filled with glacial debris, is crooked as a dog's hind leg. At certain times of the year it may appear to be somewhat trivial and even dusty. But during the spring thaws it gets right down to business and runs bank full.

One of the best fords across the river in this part of Montana lies a few miles northeast of here. It was used by the Indians to reach favorite buffalo range in the Big Bend country. Although used by other tribes it became known to the whites as the Cree Crossing.

There are many glacial boulders in this vicinity on which ancient Indian carvings are found.

100. Sleeping Buffalo Rock
U.S. 2, MP 490, east of Malta

On the crest of a ridge near the Cree Crossing of the Milk River is a group of glacial boulders which from a distance resemble a herd of sleeping buffalo.

They were held sacred by the Indians and one in particular was thought to be the leader. It is now a part of this monument. Some prehistoric sculptor tried to further the resemblance with crude carvings on the boulder.

The tribes have legends of the herd's origin, and long before the white men came sacrificed possessions to the Sleeping Buffalo Rock.

101. The Thomas Party
I-90 Frontage Road, MP 381, east of Greycliff

In 1866, William Thomas, his son Charles, and a driver named Schultz left southern Illinois bound for the Gallatin Valley, Montana. Travelling by covered wagon, they joined a prairie schooner outfit at Fort Laramie, Wyoming, and started over the Bridger Trail. The train was escorted by troops detailed to build a fort (C. F. Smith) on the Big Horn River.

From the site of this fort the Thomas party pushed on alone. A few days later they were killed at this spot by hostile Indians. Emigrants found the bodies and buried them in one grave.

The meager details which sifted back greatly impressed William Thomas's seven-year-old nephew. Seventy-one years later (1937), this nephew closely followed the Bridger Trail by car and succeeded in locating the almost forgotten grave.

102. Ross' Hole
U.S. 93, MP 13, south of Darby

Alexander Ross, of the Hudson Bay Company, with 55 Indian and white trappers, 89 women and children and 392 horses, camped near here on March 12, 1824, enroute from Spokane House to the Snake River country. Nearly a month was spent here in a desperate attempt to break through the deep snow across the pass to the Big Hole, and from their hardships and tribulations, Ross called this basin "The Valley of Troubles."

103. Jorgen Elesius Madson
Montana 78, MP 28, south of Absarokee—Marker no longer displayed

Jorgen Elesius Madson, Pioneer Lutheran pastor, began his ministry in the foothills of the Crazy Mountains during 1895. His circuit riding included the open range and mountain valleys from Hardin to the Snowies near Lewistown to the Belts and Beartooth Mountains. From Melville he served a wide area, traveling great distances, ministering to scattered families and communities. He organized the numerous churches of the southern Montana district.

On the opening of the Crow Reservation he homesteaded across the highway from this marker. This home he named "Fagerheim" (Beautiful Home) because of the surrounding natural beauty. From here he continued his work among the homesteaders and ranchers and in the growing communities of the Billings and Yellowstone areas until his demise January 6, 1928.

For a time he was the only Lutheran minister in Montana; under rugged pioneering conditions and at great personal sacrifices he devoted his lifelong ministry to the Land of the Shining Mountains.

104. Old Fort Gilbert
Montana 200, MP 58, north of Sidney

"Old Fort Gilbert" was situated directly east of this point on the west bank of the Yellowstone River. The Fort was named after Colonel Gilbert, one-time commanding officer at Fort Buford, and existed between the years 1864 and 1867. It was used as a trading center in the lower Yellowstone Valley. This point also marks the south boundary of the Fort Buford Military Reservation, which post operated for many years on the north bank of the Missouri River at the mouth of the Yellowstone.

By taking the side road just north of here and going west a short distance to Fort Gilbert Lookout Point, on the bluffs, you have an excellent view of the Yellowstone Valley. Well worth the drive.

105. Old Fort Peck
Montana 24, MP 59, west of Fort Peck

On the west bank of the Missouri River about 1 mile from the Dam was located Old Fort Peck.

The stockade about 300 feet square with walls 12 feet high of cottonwood logs set vertically, 3 bastions and 3 gateways on the front, and 2 bastions on the rear, enclosed quarters for men, store houses, blacksmith shops, stables and corral. Built in 1867 by the firm of Durfee & Peck as a trading post, the fort was named for Colonel Campbell K. Peck. Although not an Army post, it often served as temporary headquarters for military men and commissioners sent out by the Government to negotiate with the Indians.

To peaceful Indians it was an important trading post, to trappers and rivermen a safe shelter from warlike Indians. Stern-wheel steamers loaded and unloaded here and took on wood for steam for their journeys.

Old Fort Peck is history. Its site lies peacefully, with its memories, covered by a man-made lake which is formed by the largest earth-filled dam ever built by man.

106. Robber's Roost
Montana 287, MP 28, south of Sheridan

In 1863, Pete Daly built a road house on the stage route
between Virginia City and Bannack to provide entertain-
ment for man and beast. The main floor was a shrine to
Bacchus and Lady Luck. The second floor was dedicated to
Terpsichore and bullet holes in the logs attest the fervor of
ardent swains for fickle sirens. Occasionally a gent suc-
cumbed.

Pete's tavern became a hangout for unwholesome
characters who held up stage coaches and robbed lone
travellers. One of the road agents is alleged to have left a
small fortune in gold cached in the vicinity.

In later years, time and neglect gave the building its
present hapless look and it became known as Robbers'
Roost. It is in the cottonwood grove just across the railroad
tracks. Drive over and pay your respects but please don't
dig up the premises trying to locate the cache.

107. Lewis and Clark Expedition
Old U.S. 10, MP 3, east of Whitehall

On August 1, 1805, the Lewis and Clark Expedition camped at a point 200 yards west from this spot, on the south bank of the river facing the mouth of the creek which flows into the river from the north. Meriwether Lewis and three others, on a scouting expedition in the hope of finding Sacajawea's people, had crossed the mountains to the northeast of here and coming down the North Boulder Valley had reached here at 2:00 P.M. They found a herd of elk grazing in the park here and killed two of them. After taking time out for an elk steak lunch, they headed on upstream leaving the two elk on the bank of the river for the expedition's dinner.

Captain Clark with the expedition reached here late in the evening after a strenuous day spent in snaking the boats up the canyon rapids by means of a long rawhide tow line which had broken in the rapids immediately below here with near calamitous results. At sight of the two elk, the hungry men called it a day and pitched camp. Reuben and Jo Fields went on a short hunt up the creek and killed five deer in the willow brakes which caused the stream to be named Field's Creek, now known as North Boulder. A large brown bear was seen on the south side of the river; Clark shot a big horn sheep in the canyon and Lewis shot two antelope a short distance up stream. Near camp was seen the first Maximilan Jay known to science. The temperature at sunrise on August 2 was fifty degrees above zero.

108. The Whoop-Up Trail
I-15, MP 319, Dutton rest area

During the 1860s and 1870s supplies and trade goods that came up the Missouri River from St. Louis were transferred at Fort Benton from steamboat to wagon freight for inland distribution. In 1868, a freight trail was open from Fort

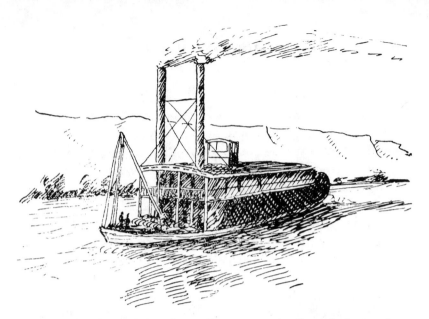

Benton to Fort McLeod, a military post in Canada located west of Lethbridge. Traders, who eagerly swapped firewater for furs, soon found themselves in need of protection from their patrons who sometimes felt they hadn't been given a square deal. This encouraged the building of "whiskey forts" or trading posts along the trail. The exact origin of the name "Whoop-Up" is lost, but one old-timer told this story: "When Johnny LaMotte, one of the traders, returned to [Fort] Benton from across the border, he was asked, 'How's business?' 'Aw, they're just whoopin' 'er up!' was the reply."

The Whoop-Up Trail was the precursor in reverse of Alberta-Montana rum-running channels of the noble experiment era. Though its prime traffic furthered the trading of headaches for hides it did gain a modicum of respectability by becoming a supply route for a few legitimate wares consigned to old Fort McLeod. The trail ran near here.

109. Rocky Mountain Laboratory
U.S. 93, MP 48 at Hamilton

In earlier days, Rocky Mountain spotted fever was a dreaded malady in the West. The first case of spotted fever was recorded in the Bitterroot Valley in 1873. Neither cause nor cure was known and mortality was high.

Through efforts of the Montana State Board of Health and Entomology, scientists were brought in to solve the mystery. By 1906 they had proved that the bite of a wood tick was the cause of the disease, which was found later to exist throughout the United States. A preventive vaccine was finally developed in this remote laboratory. Yearly vaccination of those who may become exposed to tick bite and effectual treatment methods have solved the problem.

A modern laboratory, now operated by the U.S. Public Health Service, has replaced the tents, log cabins, woodsheds and abandoned schoolhouses that served the first handful of workers. Research has been expanded to include many infectious diseases that are problems in the West.

110. The Holacaust*
I-90, MP 4, Saltese rest area

In 1910, this was a remote neck of the woods and hard to reach. Forest fire protection was relatively new. That dry summer many small fires started. Public apathy, together with manpower shortage, lack of organization and good equipment and inaccessibility permitted them to spread and join. Hell broke loose in August. Whipped by 50-mile gales, the combined blaze covered 3,000 square miles in three days. Animals were trapped, 87 human lives were lost, settlements and railroad trestles were destroyed, six billion board feet of timber burned like kindling. The pungent smoke pall stretched to eastern Montana.

Some good came from this costly burnt sacrifice to inadequate organization, funds and public understanding. Legislation was enacted, appropriations were increased, cooperative effort was developed, and the public became forest fire conscious. Now U.S. Forest Service lookouts and aerial patrols discover fires while small, then smoke-chasers by trail and smoke-jumpers by parachute reach and control most of the fires in record time. This devastated area has been re-stocked with trees that will again produce commercial timber, provide homes for wildlife and recreation for people. Fire protection methods, equipment and organization capable of handling future threats of dry summers will pay off in healthy water-sheds and abundant forest products. An uncontrolled forest fire is a terrifying, destructive beast. Please be careful with your matches, cigarettes and campfires, won't you?

*Fletcher may have deliberately misspelled holocaust to reflect local usage.

111. Maiden's Gold
U.S. 191, MP 12, north of Lewistown

The old mining camp of Maiden, now a ghost town, is located about 10 miles east of here. She roared into existence in May, 1880, when gold was discovered by "Skookum Joe" Anderson, David Jones, Frank "Pony" McPartland, J. R. Kemper, C. Snow and others.

"Skookum Joe" and Jones located placer claims in Virgin Gulch and later moved to Alpine Gulch. Several good placer diggings were opened the following month.

The first quartz mine was also located by Anderson and Jones. The Maginnis, the Spotted Horse and the Collar were the best quartz producers. The ore in the Spotted Horse was "high grade" and was found in pockets.

Over three millions in gold were taken from Maiden. Her population was 1,200 at the top of the boom. Ten years later it had dwindled to less than 200. The camp was prosperous for about 15 years.

112. Medicine Tree
U.S. 93, MP 20, south of Darby

This Ponderosa Pine has been standing guard here on the bend of the river for nearly 400 years. Somewhere, imbedded in its trunk, a few feet above the ground, is the horn of a Big Horn ram, the basis of a legend which across the centuries has established the historical significance of the pine as a Medicine Tree.

Once upon a time, when the tree was small, according to Salish Indian lore, a mountain sheep of giant stature and with massive, curling horns, accepting a challenge from his hereditary enemy, Old Man Coyote, attempted to butt it down. The little pine stood firm, but one of the ram's horns caught in the bole, impaling the luckless sheep, causing his death. A Salish war party chased the coyote away from his anticipated feast and then hung offerings of beads, cloth, ribbon and other items on the ram's horns as good medicine tokens to his bravery and to free the scene of evil.

Countless succeeding Indian tribes followed the practice until, less than 100 years ago, the horn disappeared within the tree. But the Indians continue to regard it as a shrine and even the white men honor its sacred legend.

113. The 1959 Earthquake
City park at West Yellowstone

On August 17, 1959, at 11:37 P.M., this spectacularly scenic section of Montana became the focus of world-wide attention and made modern history. A heavy shock smashed the soft summer night, earth and rock buckled, lifted and dropped. In several mighty heaves Mother Earth reshaped her mountains in violent response to an agony of deep-seated tensions no longer bearable. A mountain moved, a new lake was formed, another lake was fantastically tilted, sections of highway were dropped into a lake, the earth's surface was ripped by miles of faults, and 28 persons were missing or dead. The area is now safe and much of it has been preserved and marked by the Forest Service for all to see. The Madison River Canyon Earthquake area, located a few miles northwest of here, is an awesome testimonial to Nature's might.

114. Wagon Road
Montana 7, MP 44, north of Baker

Around these gumbo buttes and across these ridges and
valleys, the old trail wended its way between Ft. Lincoln
on the Missouri River in Dakota Territory and Ft. Keogh on
the Yellowstone River in Montana. Government mail
stages, covered wagons, soldiers, people searching for
homes, wealth, or adventure—with horses, ox teams, and
mules—plunged or plodded along this undulating trail. In
1887, one freight train of 95 wagons, each drawn by 4 to 6
horses or mules, and each loaded with civilian goods of all
kinds made up the largest train to make the trip. All were
constantly watched and harassed by the Indians, whose
lands and way of life were, by trick and treaty, being forever forced from them. With the building of the Northern
Pacific Railroad, and also the fences by homesteaders, the
trail was abandoned. A few grassy ruts may be seen on the
ridge to the southwest.

115. Old Agency on the Teton
U.S. 89, MP 45, northwest of Choteau

About ¼ mile SE of this point, a huge native stone marks
the site of "Old Agency" of the former Blackfeet Indian
Reservation. The agency was established in 1868–69 and

with unusual generosity, the whites in authority permitted Blackfeet chiefs to select the location. They chose the spot known to them as "Four Persons" because of the pleasant memories associated with it. Some of their warriors had overtaken and dispatched four furtive Crees there a few years before.

At Old Agency, in 1869, the first government agricultural experiment was conducted. In 1872 the first public school was opened for the benefit of the Blackfeet. Neither project attained notable popularity with the beneficiaries. However, that same year they were impressed by young "Brother Van," a circuit-riding Methodist lay preacher, not so much by the sincere fervor of his oratory as by his courage, skill and stamina during a buffalo hunt staged in his honor.

The Northwest Fur Company and I. G. Baker and Brother operated licensed Indian trading posts near the agency where they pursued the tolerably lucrative business of bartering tobacco, beads, and other essential goods for furs.

At his request, Big Lake, a great chief of the Blackfeet, was buried on a high point overlooking Old Agency so that his spirit could look down on his people as they came to trade.

Reservation boundaries were moved north to Birch Creek by a Congressional Act of April 15, 1874 and in 1876 Old Agency on the Teton was abandoned.

116. Indian Caves

U.S. 87/212, Pictograph Cave State Monument southeast of Billings—Marker no longer displayed.

These two rock caves in the sandstone rimrock of Bitter Creek, provided air-conditioned housing for some of Montana's early families even before Pharaoh's daughter found Moses adrift on the Nile, as long ago as 2500 B.C. The cave, right, is called "Pictograph." "Ghost" Cave is to the left.

This was an ideal primitive campground, with water in a nearby spring, fuel along the coulee bottom, shelter overhead. A lookout posted on the cliff could spot the enemy or game herds miles away.

Prehistoric tribes squatted in these rock shelters and on the slopes in front, roasting buffalo meat and cracking the marrow bones with stone hammers. The earliest artists decorated Pictograph Cave walls with enduring dark pigment. Later painters, possibly the early Crow Indians, added pictures of guns and coups sticks in red, indicating more recent occupancy.

The site was excavated as a WPA archaeological project in the late 1930s. The dotted lines in the caves indicate the floor levels when the excavations began. Four buried layers give evidence of major periods of occupation. Thousands of bones and artifacts were recovered and classified.

Since sites of this type have been found on the Great Plains, this one is of national significance. Please help preserve it for those who follow.

117. Lewis and Clark Portage Route

U.S. 87/89, MP 91, 10th Avenue South, Great Falls

To avoid the series of waterfalls along the Missouri River north of this point, the Expedition portaged their canoes and several tons of baggage, crossing the highway right here. At the lower camp, some 12 miles NE the crew made crude wagons, the wheels sliced off a cottonwood tree. The upper camp, named after the bears which inhabited the islands, was located some 5 miles SW.

The portage was near man-killing: "the men has to haul with all their strength wate & art," Clark wrote.

118. The Little Rocky Mountains
U.S. 191, MP 102, south of Malta

The Little Rocky Mountains are rich in Indian lore, tales of gold strikes and the fortunes made, stories of the days when cowpunchers from nearby cattle outfits made Zortman and Landusky their off-time headquarters, of the Kid Curry Outlaw Gang and a hundred others of the days when these towns were booming, thriving, typical western mining camps.

The future, as well as the past, of the Little Rocky Mountains, may lie underground. Since the discovery of gold in Alder Gulch in 1864, $25 million in gold has been taken from the mines at Ruby Gulch, Landusky and Beaver Creek. The names of Charles Whitcomb, Robert Coburn, Louis Goslin and B. D. Phillips are synonymous with the gold-mining days. The second largest cyanide mill in the world was at one time located in Ruby Gulch.

For the future, the Azure Caves which honeycomb Saddle Butte with crystalline rooms and passages of grandeur and beauty, are expected to make the Little Rockies one of the West's most awe-inspiring wonders.

But, in the opinion of mining experts, there is still gold in these hills. Once again Zortman and Landusky will be thriving camps, they believe.

119. Camp Disappointment
U.S. 2, MP 233, east of Browning

The monument on the hill above was erected by the Great Northern Railway in 1925 to commemorate the farthest point north reached by the Lewis and Clark Expedition, 1804–06. Captain Meriwether Lewis, with three of his best men, left the main party at the Missouri River and embarked on a side trip to explore the headwaters of the Marias River. He hoped to be able to report to President Jefferson that the headwaters arose north of the 49th parallel, thus extending the boundaries of the newly acquired Louisiana Purchase.

The party camped on the Cut Bank River July 22–25, 1806, in a "beautifull and extensive bottom." Deep in the territory of the dreaded Blackfeet, the men were uneasy. Lewis wrote, "gam[e] of every discription is extreemly wild which induces me to beleive that the indians are now, or have been lately in this neighbourhood." Lewis could see from here that the river arose to the west rather than to the north, as he had hoped. Disheartened by this discovery, by the cold, rainy weather, and by the shortage of game, Lewis named this farthest point north Camp Disappointment, the actual site of which is four miles directly north of this monument.

120. Dupuyer
U.S. 89, MP 76, north of Dupuyer

Dupuyer, a colorful frontier cattle town and 1880s stop on the Fort Shaw–Fort Macleod Trail, is the oldest town between Fort Benton and the Rocky Mountains. Joe Kipp and Charlie Thomas, whiskey traders, settled here to raise cattle in 1874 and sold their holdings to Jimmy Grant in 1877. Jimmy was killed by an Indian and is buried east of the highway.

To the west, following the base of the mountains, lies one of the oldest trails in the United States. It began when early North American natives used it as a primary north-south route. Jim Bridger and his kind knew it as "The Old Travois Trail." When white men bootlegged whiskey into Canada, it became known as the "Pondera Trail."

The refugees of the Riel Rebellion came to Dupuyer Creek in 1885 and many remained to make this area their home. The Home Ranch on Dupuyer Creek was head-quarters for the famous Seven Block Cattle spread of the Conrads and a frequent stopping place for Montana's noted western artist, Charlie Russell.

121. Columbus
I-90, MP 419, Columbus rest area

The town of Columbus is located about 9 miles west. There is probably no town (or city) in Montana that had a more spectacular career, or more hectic embarrassment in finally "lighting" on an incorporated name than did the county seat of Stillwater. From 1875, when the Country-man stage station was known as Stillwater, until its incor-poration in 1907, its name was changed every time the whims of a merchant moved his stock of merchandise, or a new business appeared. First it was "Eagle's Nest," about two miles west of town; then an Indian trading post was listed as "Sheep Dip," and it was not until the Northern Pacific built a station here in 1882 and named it Stillwater that the town's location attained permanence. Even this name didn't last long, however, as the N.P. had already listed a Stillwater, Minnesota, on their main line and the similarity of Minnesota and Montana led to misdirected shipments, so the name of Columbus replaced Stillwater on January 1, 1894.

There was just reason, perhaps, that this part of the Yellowstone was slow in getting settled. It was borderland on the north side of the Crow Reservation, and there were constant raids on the area by Sioux and Cheyenne war parties who would just as soon attack the white invaders. This ever-present danger didn't appeal to many prospec-tive home-seekers, who high-tailed it over to the Gallatin or other points farther west.

122. Park City
I-90, MP 419, Columbus rest area

The town of Park City is located about seven miles east of here. In 1882, a colony from Ripon, Wisconsin, making the trip in the prairie schooners, settled in this region. It was to be their future home, so they planted trees and made what improvements they could to ultimately beautify the little city. A section of land was donated to them, and things started off in a prosperous pleasant manner. The railroad soon came through and established a station. The bare, sandstone bluffs north of town inspired the officials to christen the place Rimrock, but not so with the persons who had planted sprigs and started a city of trees. Bravely they clung to the name Park City, and Rimrock finally disappeared with the list of unused titles. This was unfortunate inasmuch as the general manager of the N.P. resented this stubborness on the part of the homesteaders, and in retaliation he changed the location of the proposed railroad yards and shops from this townsite to Laurel.

123. Wood Mountain Trail
Montana 13, MP 47, south of Scobey

This Indian trail extended from the Yellowstone River past this point to the Wood Mountains in Canada. It was used for decades by the Sioux and the Assiniboine tribes in pursuit of the migrating buffalo. Also stalking this meat staple on the hoof were the Metis, a French Canadian band of Indians who used the trail. In the 1800s fur hunters and trappers made continual use of the passage and at the turn of the century, settlers and homesteaders followed. It was over this trail in July of 1891 that Sitting Bull and his Sioux warriors were escorted from Canada by Canadian Mounties and Jean Louis Le Gare, the man responsible for Sitting Bull's surrender at Fort Buford.

Scobey, Montana, was named for Major Scobey who served at Fort Buford and later worked with the Indian Bureau on the Fort Peck Reservation.

124. Lewistown

U.S. 87, MP 84, east of Lewistown

This area, the final hunting ground for Montana Indians, was the site of battles fought over the buffalo. In 1874 on the Carroll Trail, Reed and Bowles ran a trading post known as "Reed's Fort." Chief Joseph and his band stopped at the post on their retreat across Montana. Camp Lewis was built near the post to guard freight wagons from Indian raiding parties. During the winter, soldiers of the Seventh Infantry relieved boredom by playing cards and that's how two nearby creeks were called Big and Little Casino. Lewistown, named after the camp, was first inhabited by Metis, French Canadian Indians, who migrated into Montana and possibly gave some Montana communities their French names.

125. Beaverhead Rock

Montana 41, south of Beaverhead Rock

On August 10, 1805, members of the Lewis and Clark expedition pushed their way up the Jefferson River's tributaries toward the Continental Divide and the Pacific Ocean beyond. Toward afternoon they sighted what Clark called a "remarkable Clift" to the west. Sacajawea (or, as Lewis spelled it: Sah-cah-gar-we-ah), their Indian guide for this portion of the trip, said her tribe called the large promontory "Beaver's head."

Both Lewis and Clark agreed on the rock's likeness to the fur-bearing animal and recorded the name in their journals. They continued south only to encounter a heavy rain and hail storm. "the men defended themselves from the hail by means of the willow bushes but all the party got perfectly wet," Lewis said. They camped upstream from the Beaver's head, enjoyed freshly killed deer meat, then pushed on the next day.

Beaverhead Rock served as an important landmark not only for Lewis and Clark, but also for the trappers, miners, and traders who followed them into the vicinity. It is the namesake for the county in which it is now located, retaining the same appearance that inspired Sacajawea and her people to name it centuries ago.

126. Adobetown
Montana 287, MP 17, near Virginia City

Placer riches in Alder Gulch spawned many colorful communities. Among them, Adobetown flourished briefly as the center of mining activity in 1864. In that year alone, miners extracted over $350,000 in gold from nearby streams.

Taking its name from the numerous adobe shacks the miners constructed in the vicinity, Adobetown assumed permanence in the fall of 1865 when Nicholas Carey and David O'Brien erected a large log store. The building's central location contributed to the growth of the settlement and the development of other businesses. Stages from Salt Lake City and later the Union Pacific Railroad at Corinne, Utah, made regular stops at the Adobetown store for passengers and mail.

The town received an official post office in 1875 with Carey as postmaster. He, and later his wife Mary, served as the community's only postmasters until her retirement and the subsequent close of the office in the fall of 1907.

Once in lively rivalry with Virginia City for social and political leadership of Alder Gulch, Adobetown's population and importance waned after 1865 as the placer gold gave out in the immediate area.

127. Rosebud

I-94, MP 112, Hathaway rest area

From July 28, 1806, when Wm. Clark passed Rosebud Creek on his way down the Yellowstone, this river valley has served as one of the major avenues for development and trade in eastern Montana. Innumerable trappers and traders followed Clark's route, including the American Fur Co. which constructed Ft. Van Buren at the juncture of the Rosebud and Yellowstone in 1835. The fort proved unprofitable and was abandoned in 1843.

Buffalo hunters took over 40,000 robes from this area alone during the 1860s and 1870s, shipping them out by river boat. The slaughter disrupted eastern Montana's Indian culture and precipitated several years of bloody confrontation culminating in the Battle of the Rosebud on June 17, 1876, and the Battle of the Little Big Horn eight days later.

In late 1882, the Northern Pacific R.R. established a siding in the Rosebud vicinity as it pushed westward. Soon a town sprang up as a livestock shipping center with Butte Creek and the Rosebud forming a natural corral. Rail and auto transportation quickly replaced wagon and river traffic. As Rosebud grew it even acquired its own car dealership, the Otis Davis Agency featuring the E.M.F. line. Many an old-timer assumed the initials meant "Every Morning Fix'em."

128. Smith Mine Disaster
Secondary 308, MP 5, east of Red Lodge

Smoke pouring from the mine entrance about 10 o'clock the morning of February 27, 1943, was the first indication of trouble. "There's something wrong down here. I'm getting out," the hoist operator called up. He and two nearby miners were the last men to leave the mine alive.

Rescue crews from as far away as Butte and Cascade County worked around the clock in six-hour shifts to clear debris and search for possible survivors. There were none. The night of March 4, workers reached the first bodies. More followed until the toll mounted to 74. Some died as a result of a violent explosion in No. 3 vein, the remainder fell victim to the deadly methane gasses released by the blast.

The tragedy at Smith Mine became Montana's worst coal mine disaster, sparking investigations at the state and national level. Montana Governor Sam C. Ford visited the scene, offered state assistance and pushed a thorough inquiry into the incident.

Today's marker of the Smith Mine Disaster follows a simpler one left by two of the miners trapped underground after the explosion, waiting for the poisonous gas they knew would come.

> "Walter & Johnny. Good-bye.
> Wives and daughters. We died
> an easy death. Love from us both.
> Be good."

129. Continental Divide—Elevation 6325
U.S. 12, MP 28, McDonald Pass, west of Helena

MacDonald Pass joins two other Continental Divide cross-
ings as vital links between east and west in Montana. Both
Mullan and Priest Passes, just north of this route, had
roads as early as the 1850s. In 1870, E. M. "Lige" Dunphy
built a toll road over this portion of the Divide making
extensive use of log "corduroying" in muddy spots. He
hired Alexander "Red" MacDonald to manage the toll gate
with charges for all types of transportation except pedestri-
ans and those traveling after dark. During the early 1880s a
half dozen six-horse stages a day passed this way to and
from Helena and western Montana.

In September of 1911, Cromwell Dixon earned a $10,000
prize when he became the first aviator in America to fly
over the Continental Divide not too far from this spot.
Today a four-lane highway and an air beacon replace buck-
boards and biplanes of earlier eras.

130. E57B The Last Electric Locomotive
U.S. 12, corner U.S. 12 and Central Street,
Harlowton park

The Milwaukee Road's 656-mile electrified railroad ended
at 11:40 P.M. June 15, 1974, when Engineer Art Morang
stopped the E57B & E34C on the Harlowton Roundhouse
Track. They were the last operating locomotives of the
original 84 locomotives built by General Electric in 1915.

The electric locomotive roster had totaled 116 locomotives of 5 different types operating from Harlowton, Montana, 440 miles to Avery, Idaho, and 216 miles from Othello,
Washington, to Tacoma, Washington, over 5 mountain
ranges.

The E57B is 57' 8 ³/₄" long, 16'-8" high (panagraph
down), 10'-0" wide and weighs 144 tons. Rated at 1500 H.P.
it could develop 2395 H.P. starting effort, a 62% overload.
Operated in 1 to 4 unit consists, they were very trouble-free

locomotives. The 3000 volt D.C. trolley restricted them to a small portion of the 11,248 mile railroad and they were replaced by the more versatile diesel electric locomotives.

131. The Judith Landing
Secondary 236, MP 49, south of Missouri River

This area, which surrounds the confluence of the Missouri and Judith Rivers, was designated a National Historic District in 1974 because of its historic importance to Montana's transportation system. Missouri River steamboats en route to Fort Benton tied up at Judith Landing to buy fuel from "woodhawks." The rotted stumps of trees cut for fuel can still be seen in the area. At the Judith's mouth, Camp Cooke was built (1866) to protect river travellers from Indian attacks. In 1872, T. C. Power erected the Fort Claggett Trading Post just below the mouth of the Judith. Renamed Judith Landing, the site became a bustling community including (1885) a large stone warehouse, saloon, hotel, stable, blacksmith shop, and store. The PN (Power-Norris) Ferry provided transportation across the Missouri. The Lohse Family started (1923) a new ferry downstream, and it operated until the Winifred Bridge was built in 1982.

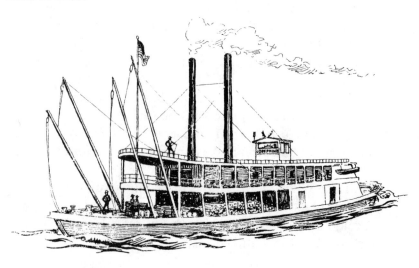

132. Fort Chardon

Secondary 236, MP 50, north side of the
Missouri River

Captains Meriwether Lewis and William Clark passed
through this area (1805) on their expedition to the Pacific
Ocean, and the landscape here remains much as they described it. Fur trappers and traders then followed them into
the Upper Missouri region. Fort Chardon was erected
(1844) on this bank, but local Indian hostilities forced its
closure two years later. The north bank also was the site of
two important treaty councils. In 1846, Father Pierre Jean De
Smet convened the Blackfeet and the Salish here to end their
open warfare. In 1855, Governor Isaac I. Stevens organized
a meeting of more than 3,000 Blackfeet, Gros Ventres, Nez
Perces, and Salish to produce a major treaty between the
tribes and the government. This area first was homesteaded
in the 1880s. Traces of early homestead irrigation systems
can still be seen within the National Historic District.

133. "The Yellowstone," by Wallace McRae

I-94, MP 65, Hysham rest area

Millions of buffalo curried her flanks
as she shed winter's ice in the spring.
In the smoke of ten thousand campfires
she heard drumbeats and war dances ring.

On the crest of her bosom she sped Captain Clark
and Sacajawea as well.
She bisected the prairie, the plains and the mountains
from her birthplace in "John Colter's Hell."

To the traveler she whispered, "Come, follow me,"
with a wink and a toss of her head.
She tempted the trapper, gold miner and gambler
to lie down by her sinuous bed.

"Safe passage," she murmured provocatively,
"safe passage and riches as well."

She smiled as the thread of Custer's blue line
followed her trails and then fell.

She carved out the grade for the railroads;
She took settlers to their new home.
Watered their stock, watered their fields
and let them grow crops on their loam.

Her banks were the goal of the trail herds;
her grass was the prize that they sought.
'Till the blizzard of '86 and seven,
nearly killed off the whole lot.

Don't boss her, don't cross her, let her run free
and damn you, don't dam her at all.
She's a wild old girl, let her looks not deceive you . . .
But we love her in spite of it all.

—copyright 1986 Wallace McRae

134. Richey
Montana 200, MP 27, Richey rest area

In the fall of 1909, a Great Northern survey crew came
through here and by 1912 all the surrounding area had
been homesteaded except the badlands. Those early years
were hard on the settlers. In spite of the survey, there were
no roads, no railroad, no market, no grain elevators and
some years no crops!

In 1911 one of the homesteaders, Clyde Richey,
applied for a post office to serve the area, and the town has
borne his name ever since. As the railroad built in this
direction, a squatter town sprouted up on the prairie and
the farmers sold stock to build an elevator. In 1916, Great
Northern surveyed a townsite and sold lots. The "old
town" merchants quickly moved to be near the depot and
the first newspaper began publication. The entire community celebrated Steel Day, Dec. 2, 1916, when the first
train arrived on the tracks, laying the last ties before it as
it came.

Great Northern Railway had intended to extend the line across central Montana into Lewistown, but World War I interrupted those plans and the line terminated at Richey. As in so many areas, the other small towns nearby died out as the railroad town became the trade center. In February, 1986, the tracks were removed and once again Richey was without a railroad.

135. Liquid Gold
U.S. 2, MP 527, Glasgow rest area

Water is the life blood of Montana. During the state's early settlement, the rivers provided transportation and trading routes; later they sustained the livestock and crops of ranchers and homesteaders; and they still provide Montana's base for agriculture, industry, and tourism. The Milk River that parallels Highway 2 from Glasgow to Hinsdale is one of the most important rivers in the north-central part of the state.

One of the earliest Milk River users was Augustin Armel (AKA Hamel) who arrived about 1820. He worked at all the major American Fur Co. posts on the Missouri River until the 1850s. In 1855, he opened Hammell's House, the first trading post on the Milk River, located about 7 miles southwest of here (near Vandalia). Tom Campbell's House followed, built near the same site in 1870. Neither lasted very long, and no physical remains of them have been found.

Later comers to this region raised mostly cattle, sheep, and wheat. They needed water on more of the land than was blessed with it and today you can see the irrigation system along Highway 2. The Lower Milk River Valley Water Users Association promoted the construction of the Vandalia Dam and Canal in the early 1900s. Area rancher, H. H. Nelson, interested in attracting settlers, became involved in irrigation after establishing Vandalia in 1904. Nelson was director and superintendent for construction of the dam at Vandalia and the canal that runs from there east to Nashua. The dam was completed in 1917. Nelson's hopes for a sizable settlement at Vandalia never materialized.

136. Dinosaurs
Montana 200, MP 248, Flowing Wells rest area

Difficult to believe now, but 80 million years ago the middle
of our continent was a shallow sea. This area, when not
underwater, was part of a hot, humid tropical coastline of
marshes, river deltas, and swamps, bearing dense vegeta-
tion probably similar to that found on the southern coast of
Louisiana today.

Fossils tell us that turtles, crocodiles, lizards, toads,
fishes, small primitive mammals, and dinosaurs lived on
this coastal plain. Many of the most complete dinosaurs on
display in the world were gathered here in Garfield County.
The first *Tyrannosaurus rex* skeleton came out of its hills in
1902. In fact, four of the six* tyrannosaurs found in the
world are from Garfield County and five of the six are from
Montana. The Garfield County Museum in Jordan holds
replicas of a tyrannosaur skull, a duckbill dinosaur skull,
and a triceratops skeleton.

Paleontologists were puzzled by the scarcity of young
dinosaurs and eggs in this rich fossil area. One explanation
was discovered in 1978 on the eastern front of the Rocky
Mountains about 300 miles west of here. Hundreds of eggs
from at least three different dinosaur species and thousands
of whole and partial dinosaur skeletons were found. This
new evidence indicates that the dinosaurs migrated from
the coast to the mountains to lay their eggs and raise their
young. One may see fossils from this site at the Museum of
the Rockies in Bozeman, Montana.

*As of early 1994 thirteen tyrannosaurs have been found
worldwide.

137. Big Sky Country
U.S. 212, MP 79, Broadus rest area

Don't fence me in,
Gimme land, lotso' land
Stretching miles across the West.

Don't fence me in,
Let me ride where it's wide
And that's how I like it best.

I want to see the stars,
I want to feel the breeze,
I want to smell the sage
And hear those cottonwood trees.

Just turn me loose,
Let me straddle my old saddle
Where the Rocky Mountains rise.
On my cayuse,
I'll go siftin', I'll go driftin'
Underneath those Western skies.

I gotta get where the West commences,
I can't stand hobbles;
I can't stand fences.
Don't fence me in.

Montana's big sky has inspired many poets. The verses
above were penned by Bob Fletcher, father of the state's
historical highway markers, which were first erected in the
1930s. In 1934, Cole Porter bought this poem from Fletcher,
and it became one of Porter's greatest hits. It was not until
1954 that Fletcher got credit for composing the famous
lyrics that inspired the hit song, "Don't Fence Me In."

138. The Bob Marshall Wilderness Country ("The Bob")
Montana 200, MP 50.5, 5.5 miles west of junction with
Montana 141

North of here lies the second largest wilderness in the
lower 48 states. Made up of the Bob Marshall, Scapegoat,
and Great Bear wilderness areas, its north end abuts Glacier
National Park, creating a continuous corridor of unspoiled
mountains and valleys that harbor grizzly bears, mountain
goats, wolverines, elk, moose, deer, and wolves.

Montana first protected part of this country in 1913 when the Sun River Game Preserve was created on the east side of the continental divide. Years of market hunting to supply miners and settlers with meat had decimated the elk herds.

Bob Marshall (1901–1939), pioneer forester and conservationist of the 1930s, was years ahead of his time in recognizing and campaigning for the inherent value of wilderness. His vision helped awaken the U.S. Forest Service to the need to conserve a portion of the vanishing wildlands from which our American heritage had been formed. Before his premature death, he had secured protection for nearly 5.5 million acres, including most of the area that was later to bear his name. Montanans convinced Congress to add the Scapegoat in 1972 and the Great Bear in 1978.

Though wilderness must be balanced with other uses of National Forests, it protects resources for us all, like watersheds, fisheries, and wildlife. Someone once asked Bob Marshall how much wilderness America really needs. In reply he asked, "How many Brahms symphonies do we need?"

139. The Pryor Mountains
U.S. 310, MP 29, Bridger rest area

The Pryor Mountains to the east cover roughly 300,000 acres. Once entirely Crow Indian territory, now only the north end of the range is on the Crow Reservation. The south end is in the Custer National Forest. The range is bound on the east by Bighorn Reservoir and on the south by the Pryor Mountain National Wild Horse Range. The

mountains came by their name indirectly from Pryor
Creek, which Captain William Clark named for Lewis and
Clark Expedition member Sergeant Nathaniel Pryor.

The Pryors hold many intriguing features, including
ice caves, sinks, and caverns, and archeological finds, such
as Clovis Points indicating human occupation as long as
10,000 years ago. In the south end of the range, remains of
log and frame houses and barns attest to the homesteads
staked after passage of the Forest Homestead Act in 1906.
Most of the settlers came from this area. Though they
cultivated some crops, for many homesteading was a
pretense for mountain grazing on adjacent forest and
reservation ranges. One forest ranger observed that some
claimants had applied for places where it would be impossible to winter over, though to hear them talk "one would
think that Pryor Mountain contained the biggest part of
the Banana Belt and that pineapples grew wild."

140. After The Roundup
U.S. 12, MP 43, Locate rest area

D. J. O'Malley grew up living at frontier forts because his
step-father served in the 19th Infantry. He lived at Fort
Keogh, near Miles City, for five years before going to work
in 1882 at age 16 for the Home Land and Cattle Co. (N-Bar-
N) for $45 a month. His 14-year tenure with the outfit
included three trail drives from Texas.

In O'Malley's day, writing verse about life on the range
was a common cowboy pastime, and O'Malley was one of
the best. His poem, "After the Roundup," appeared in the
Miles City *Stockmens' Journal* in 1893. Thirty years later, it

had become the classic, "When the Work's All Done This Fall." Here is the refrain from the original poem:

After the round up's over,
After the shipping's done,
I'm going straight back home, boys,
Ere all my money's gone.
My mother's dear heart is breaking,
Breaking for me, that's all;
But, with God's help I'll see her,
When work is done this fall.

141. The Absaroka-Beartooth Wilderness
U.S. 89, MP 24, Emigrant rest area

The Absaroka-Beartooth Wilderness, which lies to the east, contains the largest single expanse of land above 10,000 feet in elevation in the United States. The U.S. Forest Service set aside portions of the region as primitive areas in 1932, and Congress voted it a wilderness area in 1978. Visitors spent 392,000 collective days here in 1983, making it the fourth most visited wilderness in America.

Artifacts and pictographs indicate that people have hunted in these mountains for thousands of years, but it has always been country for people to visit, not live in. Reserved by treaty for the Crow in the early 1800s, the tribe shared with the less-rugged mountains on the west side of the wilderness (that you can see from here) their name for themselves, Absaroka (Ab-soar-key). The rugged mountains on the east side they named Beartooth, after one tooth-shaped peak. Gold discoveries in the 1860s attracted prospectors to Emigrant Gulch, and an 1880 treaty moved the reservation boundary eastward to allow previously clandestine mining claims to be developed.

The entire wilderness is a watershed for the Yellowstone, the longest undammed river left in the United States. It flows over 670 miles from its sources out of Yellowstone National Park and is the lifeblood of about one-third of Montana and much of northern Wyoming.

142. Wahkpa Chu'gn Meat Market
U.S. 2, MP 381, Havre

Just behind this modern shopping center is a market of an earlier vintage. Located on the Milk River (called Wahkpa Chu'gn or "Middle River" by the Assiniboine) is a communal bison kill and meat-processing camp used extensively from about 2000 to 600 years ago. This site contains both a bison jump (where the buffalo would be run over a cliff to their deaths below) and an impoundment (where the animals would be corralled, then killed). The hunter could choose the more efficient method for the situation at hand. The grazing area for the buffalo was southeast of Havre below Saddle Butte Mountain. It is farm land today, but you can visualize the browsing herds and the Indians' drive lanes leading toward the kill site.

The site, listed on the National Historic Register as "Too Close for Comfort" because of its proximity to Havre, is owned by Hill County and administered by the H. Earl Clack Museum. They may be contacted for tours during the summer season.

143. The Valley of a Thousand Haystacks
U.S. 12, MP 8, Avon rest area

The Little Blackfoot Valley is filled with lush hay fields. You already may have noticed the rounded haystacks and commented on the strange lodgepole structures standing in many of the fields. This contraption that looks like a cross between a catapult and a cage is a hay-stacker that actually acts like a little of both. It was invented before 1910 by Dade Stephens and H. Armitage in the Big Hole Valley about sixty miles south of here. The device, called a beaverslide, revolutionized haying in Montana. It helped keep the wind from blowing the hay away and cut stacking time considerably.

To work the beaverslide, a large rake piled high with hay is run up the arms of the slide (the sloping portion of the "catapult"). At the top the hay dumps onto the stack. The side gates (the cage part) keep the stack in a neat pile and make it possible to stack higher. The sides were added to the system in the late 1940s. Although the lifting of the rake is usually powered by a take-off from a tractor, truck or car axle, on some operations horse teams still provide the rpm's to muscle the hay up the slide.

Aside from minor improvements, the beaverslide has remained unchanged since its inception. Once used throughout a good portion of the northern west, modern technology that can shape hay into bales, loaves or huge jelly rolls have replaced it in many areas. The Little Blackfoot is one of several valleys in Montana where you can still see the beaverslide and its distinctive haystacks.

144. The Big Blackfoot Railway
Montana 200, MP 6, Angevine rest area

The Blackfoot River has been a transportation corridor for hundreds of years, first serving Indian travelers, then later fur trappers, miners, and loggers. The first large-scale timber cutting started in 1885 when the Big Blackfoot Milling Co. located at Bonner. The mill's principal customer was Butte copper magnate, Marcus Daly. The expanding mines created an insatiable appetite for lumber, and in 1898 Daly's Anaconda Copper Mining Co. bought the mill.

The mill started the Big Blackfoot Railway to move timber from outlying cuts to the river. The main line ran from Greenough to McNamara Landing which was on the river about five miles north of here. Logs were skidded by horses to temporary branch lines, then transferred to the main line for the trip to the river. At high water the logs were floated down to Bonner. Once an area was cleared of timber, the temporary rail lines would be moved to the next cut.

The Milwaukee Railroad acquired the Big Blackfoot Railway as a branch line about 1910 and the trains ran until 1916, when logging ceased for ten years. Both resumed in 1926, but the railway's years were numbered. Logging trucks came on the scene in the 1920s and by 1948 had dominated the industry. Hauling by rail had ended by 1957. Trucks also eliminated the need for logging camps, so most of the small communities disappeared too.

One of the locomotives, specially geared for rough track and steep grades, can be seen in the Bonner park.

145. Hurry, Honyocker, Hurry!
U.S. 2, MP 387, Havre east rest area

"Honyocker, scissorbill, nester. . . He was the Joad of a quarter century ago, swarming into hostile land; duped when he started, robbed when he arrived; hopeful, courageous, ambitious: he sought independence or adventure, comfort and security. Or perhaps he sought wealth; for there were some who did not share the Joad's love of the soil, whose interest was speculative. . . .

"The honyocker was farmer, spinster, deep-sea diver; fiddler, physician, bartender, cook. He lived in Minnesota or Wisconsin, Massachusetts or Maine. There the news sought him out—Jim Hill's news of free land in the Treasure State:

"'More Free Homesteads; Another Big Land Opening; 1,400,000 Acres Comprising Rocky Boy Indian Lands Open to Settlers; MONTANA. . . .

"'By order of the secretary of the interior, the lands shown on the map herein will be opened to homestead settlement March 10, 1910, and to entry at the Glasgow, Montana, land office.'"

Thus Joseph Kinsey Howard described Montana's last frontier of settlement in *Montana High, Wide and Handsome*. Promoted by railway, by government, and by the American dream, train loads of newcomers rolled in and filed homestead entries. They fenced the range and plowed under the native grasses. With the optimism born of inexperience and promoters' propaganda they looked forward to bumper crops on semi-arid bench land, but the benches were never meant for a Garden of Eden. There were a few years of hope, then drought with its endless cycle of borrowing and crop failure. Between 1921 and 1925, one out of every two Montana farmers lost his place to mortgage foreclosure. Those who survived learned the lessons of dryland farming and irrigation.

146. "Mining Plays Second Fiddle"
Montana 200, MP 24, Geyser rest area

"MINING PLAYS SECOND FIDDLE—FOR THE FIRST TIME IN MONTANA'S HISTORY AGRICULTURAL PRODUCTS TAKE THE LEAD." Newspaper headlines in 1910 proclaimed the change brought about by settlement of more than one million acres of Montana land. By 1922 over 40% of the entire state would have claims filed on it.

This immediate area got a big influx of homesteaders between 1900 and 1910. Many Finns settled the benchland northeast of here, thereafter called Finn Bench. Many of them got their stake in Montana as coal miners in Sand Coulee, Belt, or Stockett or as silver miners in Neihart.

Once on the freight and stage route between Great Falls and Lewistown, Judith Basin was occupied mainly by a few stockgrowers before that homestead boom. Arrival of the Great Northern Railway in 1908 signaled the end of the isolated range. It advertised "Wheat—Forty Bushels to the Acre" and "Stockmen's Paradise Has Become the Home Builders Garden Spot" to attract farmers to stake their claims here. Great Northern was motivated by its need to fill its box cars for the return trips east. What better way than to promote the government's free land to farmers who would have to ship their crops to eastern markets?

147. Circle
Montana 200, McCone County Museum

Major Seth Mabry, a Confederate Army officer, came to the Redwater Valley about 1883, driving a herd of longhorns from Texas. President of the Mabry Cattle Co., he branded with a plain circle iron. From the brand, the operation became known as the Circle Ranch. They sold three to four thousand beeves each fall for about 13 years.

Other cattlemen ran the ranch until about 1900 when Peter Dreyer and Hans Grue bought it and used it as a summer camp for sheep and as a stop-over for themselves and other ranchers going to and from Glendive. Two bachelors ostensibly cared for the ranch, but actually they started a saloon there. Since strong drink spoiled the sheepherders' work habits, Dreyer and Grue offered the place to Dreyer's brother-in-law, Peter Rorvik, in 1903. During an absence of the saloonkeepers, the Rorviks and their six children moved in. The next summer saw 100,000 sheep on the Redwater River. The herders and ranchers needed a supply source, so Rorvik opened a store on the ranch.

So began the town of Circle about one-half mile southeast of here. In 1907, the surrounding lands were opened to homesteading and the area has been producing grain as well as livestock ever since.

148. The Central Montana Railroad
I-15, MP 239, Dearborn rest area

The Central Montana Railroad used to run on the tracks that follow Little Prickly Pear Creek and the highway. It was part of the railroad tycoon James J. Hill's plan to build a vast transcontinental transportation system. As the *Helena Weekly Herald* reported: "The Montana Central was a scheme inaugurated by Col. Broadwater [of Helena] and countenanced by James J. Hill of St. Paul, president of Manitoba Railroad. Its birth was coetaneous with the decision of Mr. Hill to begin the extension of the Manitoba to Montana and the West."

Hill and other railroad magnates took the first through train from St. Paul to Helena on Nov. 18, 1887. At the very hour that locals were dressing the city in flags and bunting to welcome Hill and party, the Northern Pacific Railroad attempted to keep the Montana Central track-laying crew from building across its line. The blockage attracted much attention and a hot exchange of words, but was settled quickly; and without further incident, the

track was completed. The Nov. 21 celebration was held as scheduled.

Helenans had rejoiced five years earlier when the Northern Pacific came to town because it meant competition for the stage companies and bull-team freighters. In turn, arrival of the Montana Central broke the NP's monopoly.

The Manitoba Railway became the Great Northern in 1890 and Montana Central sold out to them in 1907. Burlington Northern now owns these lines as well as most of the others in Montana.

149. The Mission Mountain Wilderness
U.S. 93, MP 40, Ronan rest area

The mountains rising to the east lie in the Mission Mountain Wilderness Area and the Mission Mountain Tribal Wilderness. The range is more than a natural wonder; it is the first place in America where an Indian nation has designated tribal lands as a wilderness preserve. The crest of the range forms the eastern boundary of the Flathead Reservation. On the east side, 73,877 acres are managed by the Flathead National Forest; on this side, 89,500 acres are under the purview of the Confederated Salish and Kootenai (Flathead) Tribes. Both wildernesses are managed cooperatively and are open to everyone, though differences in management styles reflect tribal needs and traditions on the west side.

A few tribal elders can still trace the routes of old hunting trails through the Missions. Hunters used them to cross to the eastern Montana plains to hunt buffalo. The mountains hold sacred sites where tribal members go alone to fast and seek spiritual guidance for their lives. Other spots are traditional summer camps where families pick berries, gather medicinal herbs, plants, and roots, and cut tipi poles.

Clarence Woodcock of the Flathead Cultural Committee expressed the tribes's deep-rooted spiritual and cultural ties to the mountains: "They are lands where our people walked and lived. Lands and landmarks carved into the minds of our ancestors through Coyote stories and actual experiences. Lands, landmarks, trees, mountain tops, crevices that we should look up to with respect."

150. The Humbug Spires Primitive Area
I-15, MP 108, Divide rest area

Named for its unique granite peaks, this primitive area is part of a geologic system of large-scale volcanic intrusions known as the Boulder Batholith, which extends north beyond Helena and south into Idaho.

Humbug Spires, which can be seen to the southeast, is part of the Highland Mountains. In 1866, rich gold placers were discovered near the Spires. Most of the mining occurred on the east and south sides of the area and produced large amounts of silver, lead, copper, and gold. Total value of production between 1876 and 1947 is estimated to have been as much as $3 million. Although there currently [1987] is no mining in the Humbug Spires Primitive Area, prospecting is done on surrounding lands.

The Spires offer the finest high quality hard-rock climbing in Montana and are an excellent place to hike, ride horses, sight-see, fish, and hunt.

151. Snowden Bridge
U.S. 2, MP 666, Bainville rest area

The only vertical lift bridge in Montana is located 10 miles south of here on the Missouri River. Built for Great Northern Railway by the Union Bridge and Construction Co. of Kansas City in 1913, it consists of three 275-foot fixed spans and one 296-foot lift span that raised to allow passage of river traffic. All of the spans are Parker riveted through trusses. When completed, it was the longest vertical lift bridge in existence and had the second largest clear opening of all movable bridges in the world.

In 1926, the one-track bridge was modified by the addition of timber approach ramps and a plank deck to accommodate local vehicular traffic. A signal system regulated direction of flow and tolls were collected from motorized and horse-drawn vehicles.

No record exists of the number of times the lift span was operated, but it was rare due to declining navigation on the Missouri. The last time there was need for it, when Fort Peck Dam was being built in the 1930s and barges loaded with construction materials needed the bridge raised to pass upstream, the mechanism no longer worked. The original hoist mechanism is still in place, but the operating machinery was retired in 1943.

Snowden Bridge was closed to auto traffic in 1985 when a new bridge was built three miles downstream.

152. The Iron Mountain Mine
I-90, MP 58, Quartz Flats rest area

The Iron Mountain Mine, one of the largest and most successful quartz mines in western Montana, was located about 12 miles north of here. L. T. Jones, a former Northern Pacific Railroad brakeman, discovered the ore body in 1888. Jones and his partners, D. R. Frazier and Frank Hall, located the Iron Mountain and Iron Tower lode claims on upper Hall Gulch. Later they bonded the property for

$100,000 to J. K. Pardee, a prominent Montana mining entrepreneur, and Iron Mountain Company was born.

Intensive development began by 1889. Getting the ore to smelters was a major undertaking until 1891 when the Northern Pacific built a rail line from Missoula through Superior, four miles south of the mine.

By 1891 the company had built a concentrator that could reduce 100 tons daily. The concentrates were sent to the American Smelting and Refining Co. at Omaha, Nebraska, or East Helena, Montana, or, later, to Globe Smelter and Reduction Works of Denver, Colorado.

An 1897 state law forced the Iron Mountain Mine to close. It required all mines to have an escape shaft in addition to the main tunnel, and the Iron Mountain had only a main tunnel. From 1889 to 1898, the mine had produced over $1,000,000 and paid out $507,000 in dividends.

Later efforts to reopen the mine had only minor success and all that now remains are several wooden buildings, the railroad grade, many tramway routes, the concrete foundations of the mill, the stone and concrete powder houses, the tailings piles, and the collapsed adits and shafts.

153. The Yellowstone River
I-94, MP 192, Bad Route rest area

Interstate 90 generally follows the Yellowstone River from Glendive to Livingston, Montana. This river originates south of Yellowstone National Park and terminates when it joins the Missouri River north of here. It is the longest undammed river in the lower 48 states.

When the West was won, most rivers were lost to damming and dewatering. This river is the exception; it remains wet, wild and dam-free over its entire length. The Yellowstone flows free for over 650 miles, draining a watershed greater in area than all of the New England states combined.

In the 1970s Montanans held a great debate over this mighty river's future. When the dust settled, the state reserved a substantial amount of water to remain instream so that the Yellowstone might never be depleted and might forever remain free-flowing.

Other uses of the river—municipal, agricultural and industrial—are also provided for. Today, this waterway is in balance with all its users, including nature's creatures. Few American rivers can still make that claim.

154. St. Peter's Mission
I-15, MP 245, Missouri River scenic turnout

Approximately 10 miles northwest of here the Jesuit missionaries to the Blackfeet established their fourth mission near Birdtail stage route on the old Mullan Road. They had abandoned three earlier sites due to Indian attack or inadequacy for subsistence farming. Even this site was left uninhabited for eight years. Ironically, the same year the Jesuits returned (1874), Congress moved the reservation boundary northward, putting the Mission over 60 miles outside Blackfeet country!

To continue operation, the Jesuits converted the Mission into an Indian school for boys. Ten years later, Ursuline nuns opened a girls' school and taught Indian and white children. The Mission flourished until 1895 when the government established its own Indian schools and quit paying tuition. The Ursulines continued to teach white girls there until 1912 when they moved to new quarters in Great Falls.

A small group of Metis (people of Indian and white descent) settled on the Dearborn River near the Mission after the unsuccessful 1870 rebellion in Canada. One of them, Louis Riel, became a lay teacher at St. Peter's until some of his compatriots traveled from Canada in 1884 to ask his help in a second rebellion. Again they failed and Riel was hanged. Metis continued to live near the Mission for years, but their numbers were diminished in a smallpox epidemic in the early 1900s. They are buried in the Mission cemetery.

155. The Welcome Creek Wilderness

I-90, MP 127, about 1 mile east of the Rock Creek exit (temporarily removed)

Rock Creek, one of the nation's most celebrated blue-ribbon trout streams, is bordered on the west, just a few miles southwest of here, by the Welcome Creek Wilderness Area, established in 1977.

Not a typical wilderness area, Welcome Creek is a small enclave of undisturbed forest designated to protect an important watershed and contains no grand-scale scenic wonders. But to one retired forest ranger it is "a major island in an ocean of roads and logged areas." Welcome Creek is providing a unique opportunity to study long-term changes that logging and management produce on tree growth, soil fertility, wildlife diversity, and watershed protection. It is also a favorite summer home and migration route for about 300 elk that winter in the state's Threemile Game Range in the western foothills of the Sapphire Mountains.

156. Surrounded by Wilderness

U.S. 2, MP 141, Berne rest area

You are at the gateway to the upper Flathead River, which drains Glacier National Park, the Bob Marshall Wilderness Complex ("the Bob") and the southeastern corner of British Columbia. Two hundred nineteen miles of the three forks of the Flathead are designated as federal wild and scenic river, which means they are managed to maintain their natural primitive environments and unpolluted waters.

Directly to the south of here is the Swan Mountain Range, which stretches in an unbroken line for 100 miles. No road crosses the top of it. East of the Swan Range is the Bob.

Just around the next corner going toward the Park, you can look east into the Great Bear Wilderness created in 1978 to link vital habitat in the Park and the Bob for the grizzly bear and other wildlife.

157. Bozeman Trail
U.S. 287, MP 60, 5 miles south of Norris

In 1840, the Oregon Trail was the primary emigration route across the northern part of the United States. Two decades later, when gold was discovered west of here, a trail called the "Corrine Road" was used to bring supplies north from Salt Lake City to Bannack and Virginia City. John Bozeman, determined to shorten the time and distance to the gold strikes, scouted another route, departing from the Oregon Trail at the North Platte River. The Bozeman Trail, or Montana Cutoff, shown below, crossed here and can be seen on the opposite hillside.

This trail was used from 1863 to 1868. Sioux Indians frequently attacked the wagons and freight trains as they crossed the eastern leg of the trail. Consequently, Fort Reno, Fort Phil Kearney and Fort C. F. Smith were established to protect travelers but were also the target of Indian attacks.

158. Great Northern Railway
U.S. 87, MP 51, south of Loma

The railroad grade you see before you was the St. Paul, Minneapolis and Manitoba Railway, a precursor of the Great Northern Railway. James J. Hill, owner and builder, constructed this line in record time in 1887 to serve wealthy mining communities. There he offered more competitive freight rates to take business away from the Northern Pacific and Union Pacific transcontinental railroads.

As railroads competed for ascendancy, Montana's cities vied for transportation facilities. Fort Benton had prospered as the head of steamboat navigation and the hub of freight and stage lines to settlements in Montana, Idaho and Canada. As railroads replaced steamboats as carriers, this line by-passed Fort Benton, ending its economic importance in transportation. This line went directly to Great Falls, enabling that city to grow as an industrial and rail center.

159. Marcus Daly Mansion
Secondary 269 (Eastside Highway), MP 2, north of Hamilton

Hamilton's Daly Mansion was a summer retreat for Butte's "Copper King" Marcus Daly and his wife, Margaret. Daly came to the United States as a poor Irish immigrant at age 15. Attracted to western mining camps, he quickly learned mining skills. Through ingenuity and hard work, he made a fortune from copper and was influential in Montana's politics and economy for many years.

Daly began acquiring land to develop a 22,000 acre stock farm in the late 1880s and platted the town of Hamilton in 1890. His prized thoroughbreds, raised and trained in the Bitterroot Valley, set new records at Eastern tracks. Now open for tours, this 42-room Georgian-revival style mansion contains many exquisite Italian marble fireplaces and an elegant central staircase. Newspapers of that period termed this mansion one of Montana's largest homes, and also one of the West's most pretentious and costly dwellings. Surrounding landscaped grounds include many exotic trees and graceful flowerbeds. Other structures include a greenhouse, playhouse, laundry, servant's quarters and a heated swimming pool.

Daly's mansion is located to your left, just off the Eastside Highway.

104

160. Big Blackfoot Railroad

Montana 200, MP 32, (scheduled for 1994–1995 installation)

Railroad logging was an important facet of the history of Montana's lumber industry. The Big Blackfoot Railroad was one of several logging railroads created to sustain the Anaconda Copper Mining Company's sawmill at Bonner. Built by the Chicago, Milwaukee, St. Paul and Pacific (Milwaukee Road) Railroad between 1911 and 1936, the line was used almost exclusively by the Anaconda Company.

The company acquired 625,000 acres of timber in the Blackfoot River Valley in 1904 to provide lumber and cord wood for its mining and smelting operations in Butte and Anaconda. For twenty-eight years, the company harvested approximately 40 million board feet of lumber annually from its property in the valley—making the Anaconda Company the largest timber producer in Montana.

This section of railroad grade was constructed in 1934. By the early 1940s, however, economic depression, war and the increasing use of trucks to haul lumber caused a sharp decline in the logging industry in the valley.

Although the Anaconda Company ceased logging operations in the Blackfoot Valley in 1949, the line was not abandoned until 1978. Since the line was never intended to be permanent and was often relocated to take advantage of new timber stands, the track was frequently placed directly on the ground without the benefit of ballast or any significant grading. Portions of the old railroad can be seen adjacent to the highway on the south.

161. The Boulder River Bridge

Montana 69 at bridge south of Boulder, MP 35 (scheduled for 1995 installation)

Also known as the "Hubbard" or "Red" bridge, this structure was built by the Gillette–Herzog Manufacturing Company in 1899. The company was one of several Minnesota-based bridge construction firms active in Montana from the late 19th century to the early 1920s. This bridge was one of eight pin–connected Pratt through truss spans built by the company over a ten year period beginning in 1891. The bridge provided access to Boulder from the rich mining and ranching operations located on the west side of the river. This is the sole example of a network of roads, bridges and railroads that once existed in this area of the valley.

162. Browne's Bridge

Old U.S. Highway 91 (adjacent to Interstate 15), 1.5 miles north of Glen at the Montana Department of Fish, Wildlife and Parks Browne's Bridge Fishing Access

Browne's Bridge was constructed as a toll bridge by Fred Burr and James Minesinger in late 1862 and early 1863. The bridge was located on the Bannack to Deer Lodge Road. Joseph Browne, a miner, bought the bridge in 1865. The territorial legislature granted him a charter to maintain the bridge and charge travelers for its use. Within a few years, Browne had acquired about 3,000 acres near the bridge and had developed nearby Browne's Lake for recreational purposes. A post office was located just west of the bridge from 1872 until the early 1880s. Even though most of Montana's counties assumed control of the state's toll facilities by 1892, Browne operated the bridge until his death in 1909. Beaverhead and Madison counties assumed joint ownership of the bridge in 1911.

In 1915 the counties petitioned the Montana State Highway Commission for a new bridge. The Commission designed the bridge in 1915; a Missoula company built it during the autumn and winter of that year. A riveted Warren through truss bridge, it was one of the first structures designed by the Commission's bridge department. In 1920 high water destroyed the old structure, which was located slightly upstream from this bridge.

Beaverhead County rehabilitated this bridge with funds provided by the Montana Department of Transportation.

163. Kalispell-Somers Railroad Spur Line

U.S. 93, between Kalispell and Somers (scheduled for future installation)

In 1990, Great Northern Railway tycoon James J. Hill and local businessman John O'Brien joined forces to build and operate a railroad and sawmill on the north shore of Flathead Lake. Hill built this 11 mile long railroad spur in record time and provided financial assistance for the construction of the sawmill. In return, O'Brien supplied 600,000 railroad ties annually to the Great Northern Railway until 1906 when Hill obtained sole ownership of the sawmill. At Somers, O'Brien build 122 residences and a general store to provide housing and support services to the workers and their families. By 1910, the Somers Lumber Company sawmill was the largest in the Flathead Valley, producing over 30 million board feet of lumber annually. Freight and passenger trains passed over the spur line daily carrying travelers between the Great Northern depot in Kalispell and the steamboat terminal at Somers. The sawmill closed and was dismantled in 1949. The Burlington Northern Railroad used Kalispell-Somers Spur line until 1985.

164. A Montana Crossroads

U.S. 87, MP 55, 3 miles northeast of Loma (scheduled for 1994–1995 installation)

The Missouri River once flowed northeasterly through this valley to Hudson Bay. During the Bull Lake Ice Age, an ice dam near Loma diverted the river into its current channel. This channel began filling with glacial sediment, preventing the river from returning to its original course when the dam finally broke about 70,000 to 130,000 years ago.

Several sections of the highway between Loma and Havre follow Big Sandy Creek, which is located in the old river channel.

From this point you also have a panoramic view of the drainages of three major Montana river systems: the Teton, Marias and Missouri. To the southwest, the Teton and Marias Rivers merge near Loma before joining the Missouri about a mile downstream. In the background are the Bear's Paw Mountains to the east, Square Butte and Round Butte to the southeast, the Highwood Mountains toward the south, and the Little Belt Mountains in the southwest.

Because of the geography, this area was the crossroads for many events important to Montana history. The Lewis and Clark Expedition passed through here in 1805. They were followed by fur traders, the steamboats, the Great Northern Railway and the homesteaders.

NATIVE AMERICAN HISTORICAL HIGHWAY MARKERS

In 1989 the Montana Legislature passed a bill providing for this new series of Montana highway markers. Sponsored primarily by Representative Angela Russell and widely supported in both houses, the legislation was enacted to present Native American perspectives to themes that were not well represented by the existing markers, many of which date from the 1930s.

The Montana Historical Society worked with the tribal governments, the coordinator of Indian Affairs, and the Historic Preservation Review Board to produce the following signs.

A. The Vision Quest
Montana 66, near junction with U.S. 2, at MP 428 in view of Snake Butte

High points such as mountain tops and table-top buttes are considered powerful and sacred areas by many Indian peoples. Snake Butte is one such location, often used as a place for the spiritual rite of vision questing. The individual vision quest is an intensely private ritual in which a man or woman seeks supernatural power, or medicine. The Supreme Being grants this power through an intermediary spirit which can be a living or non-living entity such as an animal, a spider, a snake, or a rock. The devout quester may acquire powers of war, wealth, love, doctoring, or prophesy which must be used only to good ends; misuse brings very serious consequences, even death. First cleansing the body through a sweatlodge purification ceremony, the quester then withdraws to a secluded location for three to four days. Fasting and praying, the quester seeks contact with a spiritual being. The successful vision quest takes great concentration and courage. Not all quests are successful, but for those so chosen, acceptance of the power offered is a great responsibility, sometimes not without a price. It is said that those who acquire certain powers never live a long life.

Irvin Shope

B. The Place Where the White Horse Went Down

Metra Park/Midland Empire Fairgrounds, 608 6th Avenue North, Billings

In 1937–38 a smallpox epidemic spread from the American Fur Trading Company steamboat *St. Peter* which had docked at Fort Union. The terrible disease for which the Indians had no immunity eventually affected all Montana tribes. A story is told among the Crow of two young warriors returning from a war expedition who found their village stricken. One discovered his sweetheart among the dying, and both warriors, grieving over loss of friends and family, were despondent and frustrated because nothing could alter the course of events. The young warriors dressed in their finest clothing and mounted a snow-white horse. Riding double and singing their death-songs, they drove the blindfolded horse over a cliff and landed at what is now the eastern end of the Yellowstone County Exhibition grounds. Six teenage boys and six teenage girls who were not afflicted with the disease witnessed the drama; they buried the dead warriors and left the camp. Great loss of life among the tribe followed in the wake of the epidemic. Although time has reduced the height of the cliff, the location is remembered even today as The Place Where the White Horse Went Down.

C.   In Memoriam
U.S. 2, one half mile east of Frazer, across from dance grounds

In the summer of 1837 an American Fur Trading Company steamboat laden with trade goods made its way from St. Louis to Fort Union. Smallpox broke out among the crew, but the boat continued to its destination. Contact with the steamboat's crew during the distribution of trade goods exposed the Wichiyabina or Little Girls' Band of Assiniboine, starting a terrible epidemic which eventually affected all the tribes of what is now northeastern Montana. Many of the tribes had never been exposed to this virulent European disease and were extremely susceptible. The disease seemed to strike the young, vigorous and most able-bodied family members with such swiftness that burial in many cases was impossible. Ninety-four percent of the Wichiyabina or Little Girls' Band of Assiniboine died. By the winter of 1838, when the disease had run its course, the Wichiyabina or Little Girls' Band of Assiniboine were no more. The 80 remaining Band members banded with other smallpox survivors and formed the Redbottom Band (Hudesabina) of Assiniboines. Today the Assiniboine people still mourn the untimely passing of so many of their ancestors, innocent victims of this dreadful pestilence.

D. The Little Rocky Mountains
U.S. 191, MP 102, south of Malta. Tribal association:
Fort Belknap

Many Indian people believe that spirits dwell in north
central Montana's "island" mountains: the Sweet Grass
Hills and the Bears Paw and Little Rocky ranges. Their
rugged peaks, clustered like tepees in a camp, offer access
to the supernatural and provide a nesting place for eagles,
the messengers of the spirits who live there. Generations
of Blackfeet, Gros Ventre, Assiniboine, and Chippewa-Cree
have used these isolated areas for fasting, prayer and
vision questing. Here are the precious gifts of water,
plants, animals, and solitude from the Great Spirit. Stories
describing the supernatural powers of the Little Rocky
Mountains abound. One such story, handed down in
many variations, tells of a terrible water-monster called
Bax'aa that inhabited the spring on Eagle Child Mountain,
frightening or even slaying some who attempted to fast
there. Another well known site at the western end of the
Little Rockies is a battleground remembered among northern Montana tribes for its spiritual significance. The great
Gros Ventre warrior Red Whip won victory there over the
Sioux against incredible odds. His success is attributed to
a powerful war charm and a vision that foretold the
battle.

E. Old Agency, 1880–1894
U.S. 89, south of Browning at Badger Creek turnout

The second Indian Agency on the Blackfeet Reservation
was built at Old Agency in 1879. Agent John Young moved
the buildings from Upper Badger Creek with help from the
Blackfeet Indians. Both men and women dug cellars,
hauled stone and mixed mortar. The women covered the
exterior with lime from Heart Butte. Built in stockade
shape, the Agency had two bastions at diagonal corners to

protect against enemy attack. The Indians called it "Old Ration Place" after the government began issuing rations. The "Starvation Winter" of 1883–1884 took the lives of about 500 Blackfeet Indians who had been camping in the vicinity of Old Agency. This tragic event was the result of an inadequate supply of government rations during an exceptionally hard winter. In 1894, after the Great Northern Railway had extended its tracks across the Reservation, the Agency moved to Willow Creek at the present site in Browning. Today, the Museum of the Plains Indian in Browning houses a fine collection of artifacts that illustrate Blackfeet culture before and after the establishment of the Reservation.

F. Chief Mountain and Old North Trail
U.S. 89, Dupuyer North rest area

Chief Mountain, NINA-STA-QUAY, has always been known to the Blackfeet people. Identified on maps as King Mountain as early as 1796, this outstanding landmark has long been revered for its supernatural powers. Generations of Blackfeet have used Chief Mountain for fasting and prayer. In 1992, the Blackfeet Tribe, by Tribal Resolution, limited public access into the area.

The ancient Old North Trail, well worn by centuries of Indian travois, entered the United States from the north, a few miles west of present day Port of Piegan Customs. It ran along the east slope of the Rocky Mountains from Edmonton, Alberta, to at least as far as Helena, Montana.

Perhaps one of the great migration routes of early man, the Trail more recently served the Northwest Plains Indians as the route for war parties and exchanging goods between Canada and the United States. The Museum of the Plains Indian in Browning relates the story of Plains Indian culture including native travel patterns from earliest times to the present.

RECOMMENDED READING

Many of the older titles in this list are available in reprint editions.

Alderson, Nannie, and Helena Huntington Smith. *A Bride Goes West*. New York: Farrar and Rinehart, 1942.

Baker, Don. *Next Year Country: The Story of Eastern Montana*. Boulder, Colorado: Fred Pruett Books, 1992.

Blew, Mary Clearman. *All But the Waltz: A Memoir of Five Generations in the Life of a Montana Family*. New York: Penguin, 1991.

————. *Balsamroot, A Memoir*. New York: Viking, 1994.

Brown, Mark Herbert. *The Flight of the Nez Perce*. New York: Putnam, 1967.

————. *The Plainsmen of the Yellowstone: A History of the Yellowstone Basin*. New York: G. P. Putnam's Sons, 1961.

Bryan, William L., Jr. *Montana's Indians: Yesterday and Today*. Helena: American & World Geographic, 1985.

Bullchild, Percy. *The Sun Came Down*. New York: Harper & Row, 1985.

Burlingame, Merrill G. *The Montana Frontier*. Helena, Montana: State Publishing Company, 1942.

Cheney, Roberta Carkeek. *Names on the Face of Montana: The Story of Montana's Place Names*. 2d ed. Missoula, Montana: Mountain Press, 1983.

De Voto, Bernard. *Across the Wide Missouri*. Boston: Houghton Mifflin, 1947.

————. *The Journals of Lewis and Clark*. Abridged. Boston: Little Brown, 1953.

Dimsdale, Thomas J. *The Vigilantes of Montana or Popular Justice in the Rocky Mountains*. Virginia City: Montana Post, 1866.

Doig, Ivan. *This House of Sky: Landscapes of a Western Mind*. New York: Harcourt Brace Jovanovich, 1978.

Ewers, John C. *The Blackfeet: Raiders on the Northwestern Plains*. Norman: University of Oklahoma Press, 1958.

————. *Indian Life on the Upper Missouri*. Norman: University of Oklahoma Press, 1968.

Farr, William E., and K. Ross Toole. *Montana: Images of the Past*. Boulder, Colorado: Pruett, 1978.

Federal Writer's Project. *Montana: A State Guide Book*. New York: Viking Press, 1939.

Flathead Culture Committee. *A Brief History of the Flathead Tribe*. St. Ignatius, Montana: Flathead Culture Committee, 1988.

Fletcher, Robert H. *Corral Dust*. Helena, Montana: Robert H. Fletcher, 1934, 1935.

————. *Free Grass to Fences: The Montana Cattle Range Story*. NewYork: University Publishers, 1960.

Fort Belknap Education Department. *War Stories of the White Clay People*. Fort Belknap, Montana: Fort Belknap Education Department, 1982.

Fowler, Loretta. *Shared Symbols, Contested Meanings: Gros Ventre Culture and History, 1778–1984*. Ithaca, New York: Cornell University Press, 1987.

Frison, George C. *Prehistoric Hunters of the High Plains*. 2d ed. New York: Academic Press, 1991.

Garcia, Andrew. *Tough Trip Through Paradise, 1878–1879*. Edited by Ben Stein. Boston: Houghton Mifflin, 1967.

George, Susanne K. *The Adventures of the Woman Homesteder: The Life and Letters of Elinore Pruitt Stewart*. Lincoln: University of Nebraska Press, 1992.

Giraud, Marcel. *The Metis in Western Canadian West*. Vol. 2. Translated by George Woodcock. Lincoln: University of Nebraska Press, 1986.

Glasscock, Carl B. *The War of the Copper Kings: Builders of Butte and Wolves of Wall Street*. Indianapolis: Bobbs-Merrill, 1935.

Graves, F. Lee. *Montana's Fur Trade Era*. Helena, Montana: American & World Geographic, 1994.

Grinnell, George Bird. *Blackfoot Lodge Tales: The Story of a Prairie People*. Lincoln: University of Nebraska Press, 1962.

Guthrie, A. B., Jr. *The Big Sky*. Boston: Houghton Mifflin, 1947.

Haines, Aubrey. *An Elusive Victory: The Battle of the Big Hole*. West Glacier: Glacier Natural History Association, 1991.

Hedren, Paul L. *The Great Sioux War 1876–77*. Helena, Montana: Montana Historical Society Press, 1991.

Howard, Ella Mae. *Lewis and Clark Exploration of Central Montana*. Great Falls, Montana: Lewis and Clark Interpretive Association, 1993.

Howard, Joseph Kinsey. *Montana, High, Wide and Handsome*. New Haven, Connecticut: Yale University Press, 1943.

———. *Montana Margins: A State Anthology*. New Haven, Connecticut: Yale University Press, 1946.

———. *Strange Empire: A Narrative of the Northwest*. New York: William Morrow, 1952.

Kammen, Lefthand, Frederick Lefthand, and Joe Marshall. *Soldiers Falling into Camp: The Battles at the Rosebud and the Little Big Horn*. Encampment, Wyoming: Affiliated Writers of America, 1992.

Killoren, John J. *"Come Blackrobe": DeSmet and the Indian Tragedy*. Norman: University of Oklahoma Press, 1994.

Kittredge, William, and Annick Smith, eds. *The Last Best Place: A Montana Anthology*. Helena: Montana Historical Society Press, 1988.

Kootenai Culture Committee. *Kootenai Legends*. Elmo, Montana: Kootenai Culture Committee, 1984.

Lang, William L., and Rex C. Myers. *Montana: Our Land and People*. 2d ed. Boulder, Colorado: Pruett, 1979.

Lass, William E. *A History of Steamboating on the Upper Missouri*. Lincoln: University of Nebraska Press, 1962.

Linderman, Frank Bird. *American: The Life Story of a Great Indian, Plenty-Coups, Chief of the Crows*. New York: John Day Company, 1930.

———. *Kootenai Why Stories*. New York: Charles Scribner's Sons, 1926.

———. *Montana Adventure*. Edited by H. G. Merriam. Lincoln: University of Nebraska Press, 1968.

Long, James L. (First Boy). *Land of Nakota, The Story of the Assiniboine Indians*. Helena, Montana: State Publishing Company, 1942.

Long Standing Bear Chief. *Ni-Kso-Ko-Wa: Blackfoot Spirituality, Traditions, Values, and Beliefs*. Browning, Montana: Spirit Talk Press, 1992.

Maclean, Norman. *A River Runs Through It and Other Stories*. Chicago: University of Chicago Press, 1976.

Madsen, Brigham D. and Betty M. Madsen. *North to Montana: Jehus, Bullwhackers, and Mule Skinners on the Montana Trail*. Salt Lake City: University of Utah, 1980.

Malone, Michael P. *The Battle for Butte: Mining and Politics on Northern Frontiers, 1864–1906*. Seattle: Unversity of Washington Press, 1981.

Malone, Michael P., Richard B. Roeder, and William L. Lang. *Montana: A History of Two Centuries*. 2d ed. Seattle: University of Washington Press, 1991.

McCarter, Steve. *Guide to the Milwaukee Road in Montana*. Helena: Montana Historical Society, 1992;

Medicine Crow, Joseph. *From the Heart ofthe Crow Country: The Crow Indians Own Stories*. New York: Orion Books, 1992.

Miller, Don C., and Stan B. Cohen. *Military and Trading Posts of Montana*. Missoula, Montana: Pictorial Histories, 1978.

Montana Historical Society. *Montana The Magazine of Western History*. 1951—. Also see Douglas J. Easton. *Montana The Magazine of Western History Comprehensive Index, 1951–1990*. Helena, 1993.

————. *Not in Precious Metals Alone: A Manuscript History of Montana*. Helena: Montana Historical Society Press, 1976.

Montana Archaelogical Society. *Archaelology in Montana.* 1958—.

Moulton, Gary E. *The Journals of the Lewis and Clark Expedition.* 8 vols. Lincoln: University of Nebraska Press, 1983–1993.

Myers, Rex C. *Lizzie: The Letters of Elizabeth Chester Fisk, 1864–1893.* Missoula, Montana: Mountain Press, 1989.

Nasatir, A. P. *Before Lewis and Clark.* 2 vols. Lincoln: University of Nebraska Press, 1990.

Peavy, Linda, and Ursula Smith. *The Gold Rush Widows of Little Falls: A Story Drawn from the Letters of Pamelia and James Fergus.* St. Paul: Minnesota Historical Society, 1990.

Phillips, Paul C., ed. *Forty Years on the Frontier, As Seen in the Journals and Reminiscences of Granville Stuart.* 2 vols. Cleveland: Arthur H. Clark, 1925.

———. *The Fur Trade.* 2 vols. Norman: University of Oklahoma Press, 1961.

Powell, Peter. *People of the Sacred Mountain: A History of the Northern Cheyenne Chiefs and Warrior Societies, 1830–1879, With an Epilogue, 1969–1974.* New York: Harper and Row, 1979.

Rocky Boy School. *Chippewa and Cree.* Rocky Boy, Montana: Rocky Boy School, 1977.

Ronda, James P. *Lewis and Clark among the Indians.* Lincoln: University of Nebraska Press, 1984.

Russell, Charles M. *Trails Plowed Under.* Garden City, New York: Doubleday, 1927.

Sharp, Paul Frederick. *Whoop-up Country: The Canadian-American West, 1865–1885.* Minneapolis: University of Minnesota Press, 1955.

Shope, Richard, ed. *Irvin Shope Drawings and Paintings*. Helena, Montana: Privately printed, 1987.

Shoulderblade, James et. al. *Naevahoo'ohtseme=We are going back home: Cheyenne History and Stories*. Edited by Wayne Leman. Winnipeg, Ontario: Algonquian and Iroquoian Linguistics, 1987.

Sievert, Ken, and Ellen Sievert. *Virginia City and Alder Gulch*. Helena: American & World Geographic, 1993.

Spence, Clark C. *Territorial Politics and Government in Montana, 1864–1889*. Urbana: University of Illinois Press, 1975

Stegner, Wallace. *Wolf Willow*. New York: Viking Press, 1955.

Sunder, John E. *The Fur Trade on the Upper Missouri, 1840–1865*. Norman: University of Oklahoma Press, 1965.

Swartout Robert R., Jr., and Harry W. Fritz. *The Montana Heritage: An Anthology of Historical Essays*. Helena, Montana: Montana Historical Society Press, 1992.

Tirrell, Norma. *Montana*. Oakland, California: Compass America Guides, 1991.

Toole, K. Ross. *Montana: An Uncommon Land*. Norman: University of Oklahoma Press, 1959.

———. *The Rape of the Great Plains: Northwest America, Cattle and Coal*. Boston: Little Brown and Company 1976.

———. *Twentieth Century Montana: A State of Extreme*. Norman: University of Oklahoma Press, 1972.

Two Leggins. *Two Leggins, The Making of a Crow Warrior*. Edited by Peter Nabokov. New York: Crowell, 1967.

Utley, Robert M. *Last Days of the Sioux Nation*. New Haven: Yale University Press, 1963.

Van Cleve, Spike. *Forty Years' Gatherin's*. Kansas City, Missouri: Lowell Press, 1977.

Vichorek, Daniel N. *The Hi-Line: Profiles of a Montana Land*. Helena, Montana: American & World Geographic Publishing, 1993.

————. *Montana's Homestead Era*. Helena: American & World Geographic, 1987.

Vine, Bob. *Women of the Washoe: Anaconda's First Smelterwomen*. N.p., 1989.

Walker, Mildred. *Winter Wheat*. Lincoln: University of Nebraska Press, 1944.

Weist, Tom. *A History of the Cheyenne People*. Billings: Montana Council for Indian Education, 1977.

Welch, James. *Winter in the Blood*. New York: Harper & Row, 1974.

————. *Fools Crow*. New York: Viking, 1987.

Wessel, Thomas R. *A History of the Rocky Boy's Reservation*. Bozeman: Montana State University, 1974.

West, Carroll Van. *A Traveler's Companion to Montana History*. Helena: Montana Historical Society Press, 1986.

Wilfong, Cheryl. *Following the Nez Perce Trail*. Corvallis: Oregon State University Press, 1990.

Wolle, Muriel. *Montana Pay Dirt: A Guide to the Mining Camps of the Treasure State*. Denver: Sage Books, 1963/1982.

Woodcock, Clarence, ed. *Stories from Our Elders*. St. Ignatius, Montana: Flathead Culture Committee, 1979.

Yellowtail: Crow Medicine Man and Sun Dance Chief, An Autobiography. As told to Michael Oren Fitzgerald. Norman: University of Oklahoma Press, 1991.

INDEX

A

Absaroka-Beartooth Wilderness Area, 90
Absarokee, 62
Adams, Thomas, 7
Adobetown, 78, 79
Aiken, Alexander, 59
Alder, 51
Alder Gulch, 20, 24, 52, 54, 73, 78, 79
Allison, William, 46
American Fur Company, 22, 28, 31, 40, 79, 85, 110, 111
Anaconda, 59, 105
Anaconda Copper Mining Company, 59, 92, 105
Anderson, Reece, 7
Anderson, "Skookum Joe", 68
Angevine, 92
Arapaho Indians, 14, 38
Arlee, 52, 53
Armel, Augustin, 85
Armitage, H., 91
Armstead, 54
Assiniboine Indians, 31, 38, 39, 40, 42, 43, 76, 91, 111, 112
Atlantic Cable Quartz Lode, 59
Augusta, 51
Avon, 96
Azure Caves, 77

B

Bad Rock Canyon, 60
Bainville, 31, 102
Baker, 70
Baker, I. G., 71
Bannack, 24, 25, 30, 48, 64, 103, 106
Barrett, 24
Basin, 49
Battle of the Bears Paw, 37, 49
Battle of the Big Hole, 50
Battle of the Little Big Horn, 17, 18, 19, 31, 39, 47, 79
Battle of the Rosebud, 79
Bear Tooth, 3
Bearmouth, 25
Bears Paw Mountains, 37, 108, 112
Beartooth Mountains, 35, 62, 90
Beartown, 25
Beaver Creek, 73

126

Browning, 44, 73, 112, 113, 114
Burlington Northern Railroad, 97, 107
Burr, Fred, 106
Butte, 46, 49, 80, 92, 104, 105

C

Cache Creek, 53
Calamity Jane, 16
Camp Baker, See Fort Logan
Camp Cooke, 82
Camp Disappointment, 73, 74
Camp Fortunate, 26
Camp Lewis, 77
Campbell's House, 85
Canyon Ferry Lake, 10
Carey, Nicholas, 79
Carroll Trail, 34, 77
Castle Mountains, 56, 57
Charlot, 53
Chester, 41
Cheyenne Indians, 14, 17, 19, 27, 31, 37, 44, 47, 50
Chicago, Milwaukee, St. Paul and Pacific Railroad. *See* Milwaukee Road
Chief Mountain, 113
Chinook, 37
Chippewa Indians, 37, 112
Choteau, 5, 70
Circle, 95, 96
Clark, Captain William, 8, 10, 11, 12, 14, 15, 16, 17, 18, 19, 25, 26, 27, 28, 29, 33, 36, 50, 51, 54, 55, 65, 73, 77, 78, 79, 83, 89
Clark, William Andrews, 60
Clark Canyon Reservoir, 54
Clark Fork of the Columbia, 7, 9, 25, 29
Clark's Fork of the Yellowstone, 36
Clinton, Major William, 47
Coburn, Robert, 73
Coloma, 25
Colter, John, 10, 16, 35, 83
Columbia Falls, 56
Columbus, 75, 76
Confederate Gulch, 10, 56
Confederated Salish and Kootenai Tribes, 33, 97
Cooke City, 53
Cooke, Jay, 53
Coover, Tom, 12
Corrine Road, 103
Crazy Horse, 31
Crazy Mountains, 57, 62
Cree Indians, 37, 61, 71, 112
Cree Crossing, 60
Crow Indians, 12, 19, 22, 35, 38, 42, 43, 47, 72, 88, 90, 110
Crow Agency, 47
Crow Indian Reservation, 15, 62, 75, 88

Custer, General George A., 17, 18, 19, 31, 37, 39, 47, 84
Custer National Forest, 88
Cut Bank River, 74

D

Daly, Marcus, 59, 92, 104
Daly, Pete, 64
Darby, 62, 68
De Smet, Pierre Jean, 25, 55, 83
Dearborn River, 101
Deer Lodge, 7, 30, 106
Deer Lodge River, 25
Deer Lodge Valley, 30
Dell, 21
Diamond City, 10
Dillon, 26, 30, 54
Dixon, Cromwell, 81
Dreyer, Peter, 95
Dunphy, E. M. "Lige", 81
Dupuyer, 6, 74, 113
Dupuyer Creek, 75
Durfee & Peck Company, 40, 63
Dutton, 65

E

Eagle Child Mountain, 112
East Helena, 100
Ekalaka, 43, 44
Elk River, 16
Elkhorn Mountains, 10
Emigrant, 90
Emigrant Gulch, 48, 90
Ennis, 32
Eureka, 59

F

Far West, 17
Fields Creek, 55
Fields, Jo, 65
Fields, Reuben, 65
Finlay, Francois, 7
Finlay, Jacco (Jacques) Raphael, 52
Fisk, Captain James L., 33
Fisk Expedition. *See* Northern Overland Expedition
Flathead Indians, 8, 25, 29, 30, 47, 52, 53, 55, 56, 98
Flathead Lake, 56, 107
Flathead Indian Reservation, 55, 56, 97
Flathead River, 102
Flathead Valley, 107
Fletcher, Bob, 87
Flint Creek, 59, 60

G

Jefferson River, 11, 54, 77
Jefferson Valley, 54
Jocko Valley, 52
Jones, David, 68
Jones, L. T., 99
Jordan, 42, 86
Joseph, Chief, 36, 37, 48, 50, 53, 77
Judith Basin, 34, 57, 95
Judith Landing, 82
Judith Mountains, 58
Judith River, 33, 82
Junction City, 15

K

Kalispel Indians, 33, 55
Kalispell, 107
Kalispell-Somers Railroad Spur Line, 107
Kemper, J. R., 68
Kid Curry, 36, 73
King Mountain, 113
Kipp, James, 28
Kipp, Joe, 74
Kootenai Indians, 6, 33, 52, 55, 56, 97
Kootenai River, 56, 59

L

Landusky, 73
Last Chance Gulch, 20, 47
Laurel, 76
Le Gare, Jean Louis, 76
Lewis and Clark Expedition, 3, 4, 5, 6, 8, 10, 11, 12, 14, 15, 16, 18, 19, 22, 24, 25, 26, 28, 29, 33, 36, 39, 40, 44, 50, 51, 54, 55, 65, 72, 74, 77, 78, 89, 108
Lewis, Meriwether, 3, 4, 6, 8, 26, 27, 54, 55, 65, 74, 83
Lewistown, 34, 57, 62, 68, 77, 85, 95
Libby, 56
Lisa, Manuel, 16
Little Belt Mountains, 34, 108
Little Blackfoot River, 92
Little Blackfoot Valley, 91
Little Prickly Pear Creek, 96
Little Rocky Mountains, 73, 112
Livingston, 12, 14, 100
Lolo Creek, 26
Lolo Pass, 27
Loma, 28, 103, 107, 108

M

Mabry, Major Seth, 95
MacDonald, Alexander "Red", 81
MacDonald Pass, 6, 81
Madison River, 32, 69

Nez Perce Indians, 6, 8, 33, 36, 37, 47, 48, 50, 53, 55, 83
North West Fur Company, 29, 71
Northern Overland Expedition, 32
Northern Pacific Railroad, 15, 70, 75, 76, 79, 96, 97, 99, 100, 104

O

O'Brien, David, 79
O'Brien, John, 107
O'Malley, D. J., 89
Old Agency, 70, 71, 112, 113
Old North Trail, 113
Oregon Trail, 13, 30, 35, 103
Oro Fino, 20
Otis Davis Agency, 80
Owen, John, 26

P

Pardee, J. K., 100
Park City, 14, 76
Pearson, John B., 59
Peck, Colonel Campbell K., 40, 63
Pend d'Oreille, 33, 55
Pershing, General, 37
Phillips, B. D., 73
Pictograph Cave, 72
Piegan Indians, 6, 44, 45, 57, 113
Pig-eye Basin, 34
Place Where the White Horse Went Down, 110, 111
Plenty Coups, 48
Plummer, Henry, 25
Pompey's Pillar, 15
Poplar, 39
Poplar River, 40
Port of Piegan, 113
Powder River, 18, 44, 49, 50
Power, T. C., 82
Power-Norris Ferry, 82
Prickly Pear Creek, 33
Priest Pass, 81
Prospect Creek, 29
Pryor Mountain National Wild Horse Range, 88
Pryor Mountains, 88
Pryor, Sergeant Nathaniel, 89

R

Rattlesnake Creek, 30
Ravalli, 55
Ravalli, Father Anthony, 26
Raynold's Pass, 32
Raynolds, Captain W. F., 32
Red Bridge, 105. *See also* Hubbard Bridge

Red Cloud, 14, 27, 44
Red Lodge, 35, 80
Red Whip, 112
Redbottom Band, 111
Redrock, 21
Redwater River, 96
Redwater Valley, 95
Reed's Fort, 58, 77
Reno, Major Marcus A., 17, 19, 31
Richey, 84, 85
Richey, Clyde, 84
Riel, Louis, 101
Riel Rebellion, 75, 101
Robber's Roost, 64
Rock Creek, 102
Rocky Boy's Indian Reservation, 37, 94
Rocky Mountain Fur Company, 35, 48
Rocky Mountain Laboratory, 66
Ronan, 97
Rorvik, Peter, 96
Rosebud, 17, 79, 80
Rosebud Creek, 79, 80
Rosebud River, 17, 19, 79
Ross, Alexander, 62
Ross' Hole, 62
Round Butte, 108
Roundup, 58
Ruby Gulch, 73
Ruby River, 51, 54
Ruby Valley, 51
Russell, Charley M., 34, 75
Russell, David H., 44

S

Sacajawea, 10, 11, 12, 14, 19, 26, 51, 54, 65, 77, 78, 83
Sacrifice Cliff, 15
Saddle Butte, 73, 91
Salish Indians, 33, 55, 56, 69, 83, 97
Saltese, 9, 67
Sand Coulee, 94
Sanderville, Richard, 45
Sapphire Mountains, 102
Scapegoat Wilderness Area, 87, 88
Scobey, 76
Scott, General Hugh L., 45
Scott, Jas. Brewer, 57
Selish House, 29
Shelby, 41
Sheridan, 64
Shields, John, 51
Shields River Valley, 51
Shoshone Indians, 6, 10, 11, 12, 26, 51, 54

Sidney, 63
Signal Butte, 18
Silver Bow Creek, 25
Sioux Indians, 14, 17, 19, 27, 31, 37, 38, 39, 40, 42, 43, 44, 47, 50, 75, 76, 103, 112
Sitting Bull, 31, 42, 44, 76
Sleeping Buffalo Rock, 61
Smallpox, 110, 111
Smith Mine, 80
Smith River Valley, 56
Snake Butte, 109
Snake Creek, 37
Snow, C., 68
Snowden Bridge, 99
Soda Butte Creek, 53
Somers Lumber Company, 107
Spokane, 55
Spokane House, 62
Square Butte, 108
St. Ignatius, 25, 30, 33
St. Mary's Mission, 25, 55
St. Michael's, 60
St. Paul, Minneapolis and Manitoba Railway, 103
St. Peter, 110
St. Peter's Mission, 101
Stephens, Dade, 91
Stevens, Governor Isaac I., 83
Stevensville, 25
Stockett, 94
Stough, Jonas, 59
Stuart, Granville, 7
Stuart, James, 7
Sun River, 4, 47, 51
Sun River Game Preserve, 88
Swan Mountain Range, 102
Sweet Grass Hills, 41, 112

T

Targhee Pass, 48
Terry, General Alfred H., 17, 47
Teton River, 70, 71, 108
Thomas, Charlie, 74
Thomas, William, 61
Thompson, David, 29
Thompson Falls, 29
Three Buttes, 41
Three Forks, 10, 26, 54
Threemile Game Range, 102
Tobacco Plains, 59
Tongue River, 15, 18, 19, 22
Townsend, 10
Traveler's Rest, 26, 27
Twin Bridges, 54

Two Bits Gulch, 41
Two Dot, 57
Two Medicine Creek, 6
Two Moons, 31

U

Union Pacific Railroad, 79, 104

V

Vandalia, 85
Vandalia Dam and Canal, 85
Vaughn, 4
Verendrye, Pierre de la, 44
Vigilantes, 25, 43, 52
Virginia City, 11, 12, 16, 24, 51, 53, 54, 64, 78, 79, 103
Vision Quest, 109, 112

W

Wahkpa Chu'gn Bison Kill, 91
Washoe Smelter, 59
Water-monster, 112
Welcome Creek Wilderness Area, 102
West Yellowstone, 48, 69
Whitcomb, Charles, 73
White, John, 24
White Sulphur Springs, 56, 57
Whitehall, 55, 65
Whoop-Up Trail, 65, 66
Wibaux, 20
Wibaux, Pierre, 20
Wilsall, 51
Wisdom River, 50
Wolf Point, 40
Wood, Maria, 28
Wood Mountain Trail, 76
Woodcock, Clarence, 98

Y

Yellowstone, 31
Yellowstone City, 48
Yellowstone County Exhibition, 111
Yellowstone National Park, 10, 17, 35, 90, 100
Yellowstone River, 5, 10, 12, 14, 15, 16, 17, 18, 19, 22, 27, 31, 36, 45, 47, 51, 53, 54, 55, 63, 70, 75, 76, 79, 83, 90, 100
Yellowstone Valley, 19, 63
Yogo Gulch, 34

Z

Zortman, 73